David Welton, DMin

The Treatment of Bipolar Disorder in Pastoral Counseling

Community and Silence

Pre-publication
REVIEWS,
COMMENTARIES,
EVALUATIONS . . .

"Dr. David Welton does a masterful job of conducting a choir of expert voices drawn from many disciplines, and he demonstrates that an ensemble of voices is infinitely richer than a few highly talented soloists. But when all was said and done, the most important lesson I learned form reading this book from cover to cover is the healing role of silence for one who suffers from bipolar disorder. Why silence is so vitally important is because the sufferer in the manic phase tires of the noise inside the head and the racing thoughts that confuse the mind, and in the depressive phase welcomes the kind of human community that makes itself felt not in conversational chatter but through quiet, thoughtful, and prayerful presence. This is a book about the healing gifts of silence and community, and the way in which they reinforce one another. Even more, though, it is a book about love, which, after all, is not 'a noisy gong or a clanging cymbal,' but the human capacity to bear, believe, hope, and endure all things, including the devastating illness of bipolar disorder.

Dr. Welton writes as one who has personally experienced bipolar disorder and as one who has been a pastoral counselor to other sufferers and their families. He testifies to the essential role played by a pastoral counselor in enabling him to function in his work and to care for his family. This book, therefore, is a tribute to those who have chosen this form of Christian ministry, to the unsung heroes and heroines who work quietly behind closed doors. Who enable others to commune with themselves and, in so doing, to create an inner community out of the cacophony of voices that have wrestled with one another for too long, and at too much expense to self and others."

Donald Capps
Professor of Pastoral Psychology,
Princeton Theological Seminary

More pre-publication
REVIEWS, COMMENTARIES, EVALUATIONS . . .

"David Welton has courageously drawn upon his own struggle with bipolar disorder in formulating the questions that he explores in this groundbreaking book. He challenges pastoral counselors and other pastoral caregivers to consider the vital role they can play in the care of those who suffer from this major mental illness. He asks readers to remember that bipolar sufferers are human beings who, even with good medical treatment, experience ongoing mental anguish; wrestle with questions of meaning in the context of their illness; and long for a secure place in community with other people. Dr. Welton has learned much from Quaker thought and practice, including the discipline of silence in the context of community. I found his account of Quaker traditions in the care of the mentally ill to be particularly enlightening and suggestive."

David C. Verner, PhD
Pastoral Counselor,
Triangle Pastoral Counseling,
Raleigh, NC

"This is a book by a pastoral counselor, for pastoral counselors. In the introduction, Dr. Welton welcomes the reader into the world of his own experience of bipolar disorder, sharing a glimpse of his work with a Quaker pastoral counselor. His personal account prepares the reader for the provocative book that unfolds.

This book is organized around the themes of community and silence, and is grounded in Dr. Welton's Christian theological heritage, his primary theoretical orientation as a family therapist, and his multidisciplinary understanding of bipolar disorder. From this core of understanding, Dr. Welton applies current pastoral counseling theory to the treatment of bipolar disorder, and provides a superb account of Quaker treatment of the mentally ill that has heretofore received too little attention in the literature. Theological themes of silence and silent prayer, the Pauline notion of 'kenosis' as a way toward health, the community in treatment, and God's solidarity with those who suffer are integrated into his description of theory and practice. This is an excellent introduction to bipolar disorder and its treatment in pastoral counseling."

David M. Franzen, MDiv, ThM, DMin
Director of the Pastoral Care
and Counseling Department,
Alamance Regional Medical Center,
Burlington, NC

"David Welton's generosity of spirit toward those who suffer from bipolar illness and those who care for them radiates from every page of this remarkable book. He writes with the wisdom, compassion, and authority of one who has struggled firsthand with bipolar illness and who now, in his professional life, chooses to enter its chaos in counseling fellow travelers. By introducing into the therapeutic mix certain Quaker sensibilities concerning the role of silence and of intentional community, Welton issues a rare challenge and compelling invitation to ministers otherwise tempted to remain on the sidelines when facing those with severe mental illness."

Robert C. Dykstra, PhD
Associate Professor of Pastoral Theology,
Princeton Theological Seminary

NOTES FOR PROFESSIONAL LIBRARIANS AND LIBRARY USERS

This is an original book title published by The Haworth Pastoral Press®, an imprint of The Haworth Press, Inc. Unless otherwise noted in specific chapters with attribution, materials in this book have not been previously published elsewhere in any format or language.

CONSERVATION AND PRESERVATION NOTES

All books published by The Haworth Press, Inc., and its imprints are printed on certified pH neutral, acid-free book grade paper. This paper meets the minimum requirements of American National Standard for Information Sciences-Permanence of Paper for Printed Material, ANSI Z39.48-1984.

DIGITAL OBJECT IDENTIFIER (DOI) LINKING

The Haworth Press is participating in reference linking for elements of our original books. (For more information on reference linking initiatives, please consult the CrossRef Web site at www.crossref.org.) When citing an element of this book such as a chapter, include the element's Digital Object Identifier (DOI) as the last item of the reference. A Digital Object Identifier is a persistent, authoritative, and unique identifier that a publisher assigns to each element of a book. Because of its persistence, DOIs will enable The Haworth Press and other publishers to link to the element referenced, and the link will not break over time. This will be a great resource in scholarly research.

The Treatment of Bipolar Disorder in Pastoral Counseling
Community and Silence

THE HAWORTH PASTORAL PRESS®

Religion and Mental Health

Harold G. Koenig, MD
Senior Editor

A Theology of God-Talk: The Language of the Heart by J. Timothy Allen

A Practical Guide to Hospital Ministry: Healing Ways by Junietta B. McCall

Pastoral Care for Post-Traumatic Stress Disorder: Healing the Shattered Soul by Daléne Fuller Rogers

Integrating Spirit and Psyche: Using Women's Narratives in Psychotherapy by Mary Pat Henehan

Chronic Pain: Biomedical and Spiritual Approaches by Harold G. Koenig

Spirituality in Pastoral Counseling and the Community Helping Professions by Charles Topper

Parish Nursing: A Handbook for the New Millennium edited by Sybil D. Smith

Mental Illness and Psychiatric Treatment: A Guide for Pastoral Counselors by Gregory B. Collins and Thomas Culbertson

The Power of Spirituality in Therapy: Integrating Spiritual and Religious Beliefs in Mental Health Practice by Peter A. Kahle and John M. Robbins

Bereavement Counseling: Pastoral Care for Complicated Grieving by Junietta Baker McCall

Biblical Stories for Psychotherapy and Counseling: A Sourcebook by Matthew B. Schwartz and Kalman J. Kaplan

A Christian Approach to Overcoming Disability: A Doctor's Story by Elaine Leong Eng

Faith, Medicine, and Science: A Festschrift in Honor of Dr. David B. Larson edited by Jeff Levin and Harold G. Koenig

Encyclopedia of Ageism by Erdman Palmore, Laurence Branch, and Diana Harris

Dealing with the Psychological and Spiritual Aspects of Menopause: Finding Hope in the Midlife by Dana E. King, Melissa H. Hunter, and Jerri R. Harris

Spirituality and Mental Health: Clinical Applications by Gary W. Hartz

Dying Declarations: Notes from a Hospice Volunteer by David B. Resnik

Maltreatment of Patients in Nursing Homes: There Is No Safe Place by Diana K. Harris and Michael L. Benson

Is There a God in Health Care? Toward a New Spirituality of Medicine by William F. Haynes and Geffrey B. Kelly

Guide to Ministering to Alzheimer's Patients and Their Families by Patricia A. Otwell

The Unwanted Gift of Grief: A Ministry Approach by Tim P. VanDuivendyk

The Treatment of Bipolar Disorder in Pastoral Counseling: Community and Silence by David Welton

The Treatment of Bipolar Disorder in Pastoral Counseling
Community and Silence

David Welton, DMin

The Haworth Pastoral Press®
An Imprint of The Haworth Press
New York • London • Oxford

For more information on this book or to order, visit
http://www.haworthpress.com/store/product.asp?sku=5696

or call 1-800-HAWORTH (800-429-6784) in the United States and Canada
or (607) 722-5857 outside the United States and Canada

or contact orders@HaworthPress.com

Published by

The Haworth Pastoral Press®, an imprint of The Haworth Press, Inc., 10 Alice Street, Binghamton, NY 13904-1580.

Cover design by Kerry Mack.

Library of Congress Cataloging-in-Publication Data

Welton, David.
The treatment of bipolar disorder in pastoral counseling : community and silence / David Welton.
p. cm.
Includes bibliographical references (p.) and index.
ISBN-13: 978-0-7890-3042-9 (hard : alk. paper)
ISBN-10: 0-7890-3042-X (hard : alk. paper)
ISBN-13: 978-0-7890-3043-6 (soft : alk. paper)
ISBN-10: 0-7890-3043-8 (soft : alk. paper)
1. Manic-depressive persons—Pastoral counseling of. I. Title.

BV4461.W45 2006
259'9.426—dc22

2006007139

CONTENTS

Acknowledgments

I would like to thank my teachers of pastoral counseling, David Franzen and Carla Lang, for their clarity and passion for psychotherapy, and in preparing me for this project.

I also wish to express my thanks to my dissertation advisor, David Verner, who helped me put my ideas into intelligible English, and shares a great love for the advancement of the helping professions. His time spent on reading the drafts and offering comments has been more valuable to me than he can ever know.

In addition, I am indebted to my friends at Triangle Pastoral Counseling (Raleigh), Council for Relationships (Philadelphia), and Princeton (New Jersey) United Methodist Church for being there for me on this journey, and all those clients I have been privileged to know. Their stories have taught me of the richness and diversity of human nature, the depth of pain and anxiety that each of us carries within, and the hope that we have for finding that person inside, whom God created in the Divine Image.

doi:10.1300/5696_a

ABOUT THE AUTHOR

David Welton, DMin, is chaplain at VITAS Innovative Hospice Care in Fort Lauderdale, Florida. His professional work has included parish ministry, chaplaincy, and family therapy. His current professional interests include mental illness and faith, dementia studies, and the psychiatric dimensions of grief.

Introduction

I am a person with bipolar disorder. It has been with me since my teen years, although it was not diagnosed until I was in my forties. I have tried numerous variations of psychotherapy and medications. One therapist, a Quaker pastoral counselor, has made a difference in my recovery from this illness. I met him when I served in the parish in Florida. I had been having panic attacks, severe mental chaos, and periods of depression. I had developed a phobia about closeness with other people. I was getting very little sleep and not carrying out my duties at church adequately. I asked for a referral and was given Michael's name, and we began therapy on a January day.

After he heard my story and began to understand who I was, he realized it was very difficult for me to talk about feelings and remember significant events in my life. He asked if I would like to try a different approach to therapy, one that involved a practice of meditation from the Buddhist tradition. He called this the concept of "unknowing" and invited me to be silent and be present to my feelings. We sat in silence for what seemed an eternity; it was probably ten minutes. In that time, he asked me to allow any images that might come to mind into consciousness. I almost immediately had a memory of a childhood trauma that had significant meaning to my illness. It was a very powerful feeling and I didn't quite know what to do with it. Michael assured me I didn't have to do anything with it but accept it.

Our sessions took this pattern for about eighteen months. In that time I became a softer, more feeling person. I allowed myself to feel the depths of pain I'd had from childhood and I began to connect that pain to my current problems. I would look forward to the therapy sessions, whereas I had once dreaded the idea of psychotherapy. I embraced the practice of silence in our sessions and took on a discipline of silence at home. Each morning I would spend twenty minutes in silence before going to work, a practice I continue to this day. In that silence, using the rubric of the Ignatian exercises, I would calm the

The Treatment of Bipolar Disorder in Pastoral Counseling

doi:10.1300/5696_01

chaos in my mind and allow God's peace into it. In my work with Michael, he would add some Jungian interpretation of the images that would come to my mind and a guided way toward rebuilding my sense of self.

Although I was not "cured," I fully believe that this particular therapy gave me the best chance at functioning in my work and caring for my family (community). At this point I had not yet been on medication, and the integration of psychotherapy with silence and meditation helped me survive until I could get medical care. One year after leaving Florida, I found treatment with a psychiatrist who diagnosed the bipolar disorder and prescribed lithium and an antidepressant; I found relief from the debilitating physical symptoms of the disease.

The existing literature on the treatment of bipolar disorder, also know as manic-depressive illness, includes almost no contributions from the field of pastoral counseling. Yet through its multidisciplinary approach, pastoral counseling may be the best of psychotherapies used in conjunction with medical and pharmacological treatments. Practitioners of pastoral counseling can make use of the insights from psychodynamic, cognitive-behavioral, learning, and family systems theories for their psychological understanding of their clients. Along with that comes the work on issues of meaning and purpose, values, and religious beliefs that are the natural realm of the pastoral counselor. As the clinician is free to make use of multiple theories of human behavior, so can he or she draw upon a multiplicity of spiritual approaches to offer hope and healing to clients.

The focus of this book will be current understandings of bipolar disorder in medical and psychological disciplines, and new approaches to pastoral counseling that might be of use to the therapist. In Chapter 1, I will review the most recent research relevant to this illness, including how scientists currently understand the working of the brain in mental illness and how medications effect changes in the brain that diminish the mania and depression. I will also review the most commonly prescribed medications, summarizing their perceived advantages and disadvantages.

This chapter also will examine the genetic factors in bipolar disorder and how these have come to light, affecting the treatment of patients and their families. Most previous research has studied generational transmission of the disease and the probability of inheriting it from one's parents. Science is now searching for a "mood gene" that would shed light on the transmission of mental illness in families and improve treatment.

Chapter 1 also surveys contemporary psychotherapeutic treatment of people with bipolar disorder. Many schools of thought have contributed to current treatment approaches, including object relations, psychodynamic, family systems, psychoeducational and narrative psychology. Each will be reviewed for its understanding of the illness and treatment modalities. The chapter will end with a consideration of how these disciplines have worked together.

Chapter 2 is a study of what varieties of pastoral counseling might be useful in the treatment of bipolar disorder. Many articles in the literature ponder the interplay between religion and psychoanalysis, and these will be explored in this chapter. Research among pastoral counselors into depression will assist us in formulating a pastoral approach to the treatment of manic depression. In addition, Chapter 2 will address negative attitudes toward the mentally ill in the evangelical literature, and their potential effect on clients from evangelical traditions who are in therapy.

Chapter 3 is titled "Quaker Treatment of the Mentally Ill." I became fascinated by this topic while reading an exposé of the treatment of the mentally ill in this country by Robert Whitaker, titled *Mad in America* (Perseus Publishing, 2002). In it the author reveals the inadequacies of our mental health system, but he also reviews the history of this form of treatment in the United States. The one group of hospitals he praises for their effective and humane treatment are the Quaker hospitals founded in Philadelphia in the nineteenth century. This chapter will review the writings of Quaker reformers, such as George Fox, and will examine their methods of treatment and the philosophies behind them. Finally, Chapter 3 will elucidate some key theological ideas of Quakerism that are potentially helpful to pastoral counselors, especially those who work with bipolar disorder. The use of silence and the importance of the community of faith are two key concepts for the treatment of a manic-depressive patient.

The following two chapters address the treatment of bipolar disorder. In Chapter 4, I will review the literature on using silence, prayer, and meditation in the psychotherapy hour. The contributions of Christian and Buddhist teachers will be included. The chapter also will examine how introspective disciplines promote health and wholeness in the client. A reflective section on what this might mean theologically follows. Finally, the chapter ends with a consideration of the experience of bipolar disorder and the relief from mania that meditation may offer.

"Community in Treatment" is the title of Chapter 5. In the treatment of mental illness one must always consider the ethical implications for what counselors do, and how these are a part of the public debate and the community in which a patient receives treatment. Articles reviewed in this section address issues of quality of life, how to define mental illness, how and where care should be given, and the rights to privacy and individuality.

The realm of theology and community offers a great deal to explore. Since it is a core reality in the Christian Gospel that our faith is lived out in community, and that our responsibility is to the neediest in our own communities, then the study of the role of the community in the life of the mentally ill person is crucial. The theological literature contends that those who are in some kind of bondage, whatever form that takes, can find liberation by being in community with others. This idea of salvation in the present is what may speak to the needs of a person with bipolar disorder. Their need for reconciliation with their friends and family is critical, and the presence of a covenant community that will not give up on them may mean the difference between healing and further disintegration.

Chapter 6 will consider two ideas—suffering and healing. Many theologians have explored what human suffering means and why it exists. The person with mental illness often feels this dilemma deeply: If God loves me why do I have to live in mental agony all of my days? This chapter will examine current writing on the nature of suffering and review some classic ideas from the past. The focus here is to imagine God as one who speaks to our suffering and can be a part of the dialogue in pastoral counseling. This process may engage the client in the evolution of a new vision of God. How can our image of God change through suffering?

Chapter 7 discusses how this book may inform the treatment of the bipolar client in pastoral counseling. Our clients in pastoral counseling live the need of healing daily, and our bipolar clients, through the swings of elation and depression, seek a relationship with God that will moor them to a secure place. Living with manic depression raises one's awareness that a God exists out there, with whom we can be in relationship.

Chapter 1

Current Research into Bipolar Disorder

DEFINING BIPOLAR DISORDER

The term "bipolar disorder" is a relatively recent designation in the American Psychiatric Association (APA) guidelines. It refers to what was called "manic depression" and suggests the presence of two poles in the affective experience of the patient. Although each person has a unique pattern to his or her illness, most bipolar sufferers go through episodes of mania and major depression, either swinging rapidly between the two poles, or in discrete episodes that may be years apart. A recent article in the journal *Mental Health Weekly* summarizes current understandings of bipolar illness:

> Bipolar disorder is characterized by manic and depressive phases, and the mood swings can be debilitating. It affects nearly one in 100 people, many of whom also have other psychiatric illnesses. An estimated one quarter of those affected attempt suicide. Bipolar disorder has no cure, the APA says, but treatment can increase patient functioning and decrease mortality. (Hirschfeld, 2002, p. 1)

The experience of mania is a difficult one to describe, yet those who treat clients with this disorder can recognize it immediately:

> The patient becomes very hyperactive. He or she doesn't sleep, and doesn't need to sleep. Thoughts race, and they talk very, very fast. They may be hypersexual and spend huge amounts of money. They get in all kinds of trouble, fights, even car accidents. (Lewis, 1996, p. 27)

The Treatment of Bipolar Disorder in Pastoral Counseling

doi:10.1300/5696_02

The depressive side of bipolar disorder is often overshadowed in the popular mind by the wild ride of mania that so many patients experience, yet the episodes of depression can be as equally debilitating and often lead to suicide. During depression, people withdraw from the world and relationships with friends and family. Sufferers may lose all hope that life will get better. They may feel that going on is fruitless. They may even lose the ability to express the inner experience, so that this isolation in suffering intensifies the sense of desperation. Suicide can seem like the only remaining option (Kimberly, 2002, p. 1).

It has been suggested that bipolar disorder first appears in a patient between the ages of eighteen and twenty-four (Griswold and Pessar, 2000, p. 1343). Yet many mental health providers see the signs of this illness even earlier. In their 2000 study of children and the likelihood of developing bipolar disorder, doctors at the University of Miami studied children who seemed to exhibit the mood swings so particular to the illness (Egeland et al., 2000). They describe a young girl, Emma, who presented with bipolar disorder at age sixteen. When consulting the parents and teachers, doctors recorded a list of behaviors that may have been early warning signs of bipolar illness.

> Age 8: Bold, demanding, very outspoken.
> Age 10: Obsessive-compulsive traits, mood changes, overly sensitive.
> Age 11: Irritable, mood changes, depressed mood.
> Age 12: Bold, intrusive, demanding, outspoken. Obsessive-compulsive disorder (OCD) and somatic traits.
> Non-episodic symptoms: Energy loss, sleep unspecified, ruminations, fears, phobias, panic symptoms, worried/fearful/tense.

When she came for treatment, she had what was described as both euphoric and irritable moods, and she was often noncompliant with treatment, especially medications. When she began to accept help, she improved quickly and returned to school (Egeland et al., 2000, p. 1250).

Clearly, what patients experience with this disease hinders their ability to enjoy their lives and be productive people. What is becoming more clear is the early onset of the illness and the visible signs that family, friends, and teachers might recognize, in order to guide the person to help. The next section addresses the current ways that bipolar disorder is treated by the medical community.

TREATMENT BY PHYSICIANS

The family physician is often the first health professional to treat the bipolar patient. If he or she observes symptoms and behavior consistent with bipolar disorder, he or she must decide whether referral to a psychiatrist is best for the patient or if placement in an inpatient facility is necessary (in cases of acute mania or suicidal depression). In any event, the eventual treatment plan will include medication and psychotherapy, as well as counseling for the patient's family. As this book will attest, the involvement and support of the family will expedite the treatment and recovery of the bipolar sufferer (Griswold and Pessar, 2000, p. 1343).

In 1994 the First International Conference on Bipolar Disorder was held in Pittsburgh, Pennsylvania. The content of this meeting included issues of diagnosis, differentiation of types of bipolar illness, research into the genetic clues to the cause of this illness, and current drug therapies available to the physician. For more than forty years now the standard treatment for manic depression has been lithium, a naturally occurring salt that acts as a mood stabilizer. As the presenters pointed out, the rate of success with lithium has been good. However, the drug's side effects can be intolerable and many do not respond to it.

In the past twenty years new medications have been used with wide success and offer other options to patients. One class of drugs are the anticonvulsants, usually prescribed for seizure disorders. Two such drugs are carbamazepine (Tegretol) and divalproex (Depakote). Current studies (Friedrich, 1999; Bowden et al., 1994) indicate a similar rate of success in treating bipolar illness as with lithium, with fewer side effects. A second class are the medications that have been used are the antidepressants, most notably selective serotonin reuptake inhibitors (SSRIs) such as paroxetine (Paxil). However, other varieties of antidepressants, namely, the tricyclics and monoamine oxidase inhibitors, have been observed to increase the rapid-cycling variety of bipolar disorder (Himmelhoch and Thase, 1994, p. 6). Another researcher at the Pittsburgh conference raised the issue of "polypharmacy" or the treatment of psychiatric disturbance with multiple medications. It has been observed that some patients respond better to a regimen of two or three drugs. What seems to be the operative factor here is the atypical nature of bipolar disorder in many patients who present with the illness. The multiple-drug therapy seems to meet the unusual needs of those who may experience psychotic episodes or rapid cycling. Nevertheless, what this doctor has found is the effectiveness of lithium and psychotherapy together being the most effective treatment for the majority (Mallinger, 1994, p. 7).

In May of 2001 the annual meeting of the American Psychiatric Association took place in New Orleans, Louisiana. A substantial portion of the conference dealt with the management of bipolar disorder in the United States and Europe. European researchers raised the possibility of regular use of the antipsychotic drugs, or neuroleptics, with bipolar patients. Neuroleptics were first used in the acute mania phase of the illness, helping to reduce anxiety, manic behavior and thoughts, and psychotic symptoms accompanying the mania. These doctors have since discovered the long-term role of the neuroleptics in the maintenance treatment of the disease (Patten-Hitt, 2001). These medications include clozapine (Clozaril), olanzapine (Zyprexa), quetiapine (Seroquel), and risperidone (Risperdal) (*Harvard Mental Health Letter*, September 2002, p. 5).

The use of drugs in treating psychiatric illness has long been accepted as effective, yet the conference recognized the necessity of psychotherapy and other areas of study as well. Dr. C. Robert Cloninger of Washington University, St. Louis, discussed the "psychobiology of human personality" and concluded that personality traits had much to do with a patient's response to antidepressant medication. He further recognized that certain symptoms of bipolar disorder required initial treatment with pharmacotherapy, and then follow-up with psychotherapy. He observed that patients with anxiety, impulsivity, suicidality, and paranoia would be best served by medication first, then therapy to follow (Patten-Hitt, 2001). Dr. Ellen Frank, from the University of Pittsburgh, spoke about managing depression in the bipolar patient, and raised the importance of the psychosocial environment to the recovery of the sufferer. She suggested that patients are "vulnerable to new episodes of the disease when they experience disruptions to their daily routines or social rhythms." Psychotherapy can be the mode of treatment to help stabilize these patterns in the patient's life (Frank, 2001, p. 7).

The medical literature often addresses regarding the efficacy of the standard drug treatments, and much of the news is good. Recognizing the difficulty in treating the bipolar patient and gaining compliance with the treatment can be the hardest steps to recovery. Recent articles in both the *British Medical Journal* and the *Journal of the American Medical Association* report that lithium has reduced the risk of suicide and normalized rates of mortality. The function of lithium as a mood stabilizer has been effective, and so has its role in preventing future acute manic episodes (Friedrich, 1999, p. 2271). Although the long-term effects of the antipsychotics are not known, they seem to be most effective in controlling the acute phases of bipolar disorder and not effective in any prophylactic use (Young, 2000, p. 1). What may be most useful to the patient over the long term is the application of combination therapy in the form of drugs and psychotherapy. Early diagnosis and prompt entry into treatment is also critical. Bipolar patients go undiagnosed for many years and can relapse even during treatment. The chances for recovery are better if the disorder can be screened for and treated quickly (Petersen, 2000, p. 45).

One other medical treatment that is available to patients has been and continues to be controversial. Electroconvulsive therapy (ECT) has been used for decades, and at one time was the only treatment available for depression. The journal *American Healthline* ("Electroconvulsive Therapy," January 2001, p. 1) presented an objective look at the benefits and harmful side effects of ECT. The primary benefit seems to be the rate of remission in severely and psychotically depressed patients. The journal reported a study by the National Institute of Mental Health claiming a success rate of 95 percent, far greater than any drug therapy. Those who have protested the use of ECT, including former patients, have suffered substantial memory loss and loss of cognitive functions such as short-term memory. They also say that this treatment is violent and authoritarian. The doctors who use this method say they can't be sure if the memory loss is a result of the patient's mental illness or of the treatment.

Is ECT useful for patients with bipolar disorder? Katherine Lerer tells her story in the May 2000 issue of *Psychology Today*. Her description of the severity of her bipolar illness is vivid and frightening; her account of the electroconvulsive therapy is discouraging:

> My next memory is of wobbling back to the next room guided by a nurse. I felt confused and disoriented, like I was twirling in space. I was glad it was over. . . . The memory loss was so profound at times that I got lost just walking a few blocks in my neighborhood. The period of time before, during and after my treatment permanently vanished into the deep channels of my mind. Short vignettes are all that I have left of my four months of ECT. (p. 28)

Other physicians have written passionately about the effect of ECT on the brain and the cruelty to patients who cannot decide for themselves on their course of treatment (Johnson, 2001, pp. 3-13). It is the emphasis of this book that humane treatment of the mentally ill is our primary responsibility to our society. In some trials, ECT has proven successful in alleviating depression. To many this treatment seems inhumane. To others who have gotten relief from debilitating symptoms, it is a necessary method. What is humane may be up to patients to determine.

GENETIC FACTORS IN BIPOLAR DISORDER

In her article in the *Journal of the American Academy of Child and Adolescent Psychiatry,* Clarice Kestenbaum (2000) defines the two questions pertaining to genetic research and psychiatric illness: What are the factors that predispose one to manic depression, and are illnesses such as bipolar disorder genetically determined? She explains:

> . . . the fundamental insight of the last decade in neuroscience and molecular biology is an understanding of the way genes and the environment interact in complex and inseparable ways. The work of Hyman and others revolutionizes the understanding of normal and pathological development and links molecular biology and behavior so as to render the mind-brain dichotomy moot. The salient point in the emerging understanding of the brain is plasticity; that the ability to learn and change is brain-based, so that at any given moment there is a complex mix of one's genome and environmental interventions. We know now

> that psychotherapy and medication both act on the brain to change behavior, brain neurophysiology and neurochemistry. (p. 7)

What Kestenbaum describes is a flowing relationship between the sciences that help us to see ourselves and our world as a system. In that system are people who suffer from psychiatric disorders, and those disorders arise in complex ways. The genetic makeup of a person might be one factor of many in determining the likelihood of someone developing bipolar disorder. Kestenbaum is even suggesting that the environment and psychosocial surroundings might influence the biological and chemical makeup of our bodies, indeed even our genetic makeup. So, the question might be better put: Is it accurate to assign a predisposition to a particular illness when so many factors affect the genetic code?

Nevertheless, genetic research goes on in the quest to find the source of behavioral traits. One such study is the Human Genome Research Institute of the National Institutes of Health, which launched a three-year project in behavioral genetics. Specifically the areas include impulsivity, intelligence, and bipolar disorder. One of the emphases of the study will be the effect on the general public of such research. The questions include, "In a society of classification and discrimination, what would be the impact of genetic information about behavior? Will genetic information reinforce racial stereotypes, for example, or create new ways of categorizing people?" (Strobel, 2000, p. 47). In the past, theories regarding genetic predisposition led to the horrors of eugenics in this country, and the Holocaust in Nazi Germany. A justified reaction of fear results when we consider the ways in which society might use this information.

In a related study, researchers at Baylor University are analyzing blood samples of patients with bipolar disorder to "identify the genes responsible for susceptibility to schizophrenia and bipolar disorder" (Goodman, 2001, p. 1). Baylor is home to the Human Genome Center and has a clinical focus to its research. Their aim is to find more effective treatments for the two diseases by better understanding the genes involved. Dr. Heather Goodman says, "Clearly these are complex illnesses, which likely involve many genes interacting with one another. We are hopeful that the advances made in genome research will lead to better diagnosis and treatment options."

Neurobiologist Samuel Barondes is searching for what he calls the "mood genes" that would be the key to finding drugs to control bipolar disorder. In his book *Mood Genes: Hunting for Origins of Mania and Depression* (1998) he tells the story of how this scientific detective work is done. Journalist Jeff Minerd (1999) summarized Barondes' search in *The Futurist:*

> The mood-gene hunter first finds a family or isolated population that is prone to manic depression, then analyzes the DNA from this population to see if the people who have the disorder also have certain genetic markers. If it happens that manic depression is linked to any of these markers, the hunter knows a mood gene lies close to that marker on a particular chromosome, thus narrowing the search. (p. 11)

What Barondes is offering is a chance to treat intentionally what has until now been discovered by accident. To map out the contents of the DNA and understand the molecular functioning of the brain in a bipolar patient would allow doctors to target treatment and drug choices. It is Barondes' hope not only that treatment of current illness will be revolutionized, but that onset of such an illness might be prevented (Barondes, 1998).

Two recent studies show the patterns in families where bipolar disorder has occurred. Mahony (2002, p. 55) studied siblings with bipolar disorder and discovered that the age at which the disease appeared and the severity of the psychotic symptoms were quite similar. In spite of environmental factors, a component of inherited vulnerability exists with bipolar disorder. Wals et al. (2001) went a step further and asked if there might be a greater incidence of bipolar disorder in children of parents with the illness. Difficulties in the makeup of the samples and collecting accurate information proved prohibitive, but the researchers did find a 29 percent rate of occurrence in the twelve-to-twenty-one age bracket and a 44 percent rate of lifetime occurrence. Although the authors had hoped to find more conclusive evidence establishing a link between children and parents, they did not find enough of a statistical validation to be of value in clinical practice (p. 1094).

PSYCHOTHERAPY AND BIPOLAR DISORDER

The prevalence of success among researchers with drug treatment has often overshadowed the presence of psychotherapy as an effective mode of treatment. Two problems keep the necessity for psychotherapy on the treatment table. First, those with mood disorder still have a high rate of suicide. In the *Journal of Affective Disorders*, Angst (2002, p. 167) documented the elevated suicide rate among patients with unipolar and bipolar disorders. The bipolar rate was 12.3 percent, despite available pharmacological treatment. Second, four out of ten people suffering from bipolar disorder don't seek help for their illness. Ten Have et al. (2002, p. 203) studied the results of interviews with bipolar patients, many of whom were not identified by their primary care physician or did not seek help from mental health services in their community. Many of these patients' lives had been highly compromised due to their illness; problems included absenteeism from work, social isolation, and attempted suicide.

In light of these findings, psychosocial interventions are called for to meet the emotional factors involved in living with bipolar disorder. The truth remains that, whatever biochemical changes are wrought by miracle drugs, what has already happened in the client's life has affected their image of self and family. In many cases, by the time the bipolar client has sought therapy, they have already alienated friends and family and lost employment. Pharmacotherapy can reverse the process of the disease, but only psychotherapy can address the emotional wounds caused by the illness. Dr. Kay Redfield Jamison, the most prolific writer on the treatment of bipolar disorder and a patient as well, affirms this opinion: "Lithium makes psychotherapy possible. But, ineffably, psychotherapy heals" (Jamison, 1995, pp. 88-89).

A multitude of methods for psychotherapy with the bipolar client exists. The scope of this book will only allow consideration of two major schools of thought, the *psychodynamic school* and the *family systems approach*. These approaches to treatment seem to have been the most widely practiced in the field of psychotherapy with bipolar clients and to the most success. What follows is a focused discussion of how bipolar disorder is understood in each theoretical area and how a therapist in each school might begin treatment.

Psychodynamic Theory

The conditions of mania and depression may at first glance appear unrelated. Nevertheless, those who practice psychotherapy with manic-depressive clients know how these states are interwoven and often inseparable. Furthermore, how one defines this illness has everything to do with how it is treated. Nancy McWilliams, professor of psychology at Rutgers University, describes it in this manner:

> Mania is the flip side of depression. People with hypomanic personalities have an essentially depressive organization, which is counteracted by the defense of denial. Because most people who maintain a degree of mania suffer from episodes in which their denial fails and their depression surfaces, the term cyclothymic has been sometimes used to describe their psychology. (McWilliams, 1994, p. 248)

McWilliams here highlights the two fascinating aspects of manic depression: the intimate connection between two opposite states of mind, and the endless cycle the client experiences of flights of elation and depths of despair. For those of us who treat clients with this illness, it seems mysterious in its causes and frustrating in its cure.

This section will attempt to elucidate past and present understandings of manic depression in psychoanalytic theory, using the ideas of drive theory (Freud and others), ego psychology (defenses), object relations (Klein), and self psychology (Kohut and others). A section on therapeutic implications concludes.

Drive Theory

Sigmund Freud in his "A Case of Hysteria" (1905) looked carefully at how the earliest drives in infancy had profound influences on the rest of childhood and adult life. He reported on the case of Dora, who had symptoms that pointed back to a disturbance in the oral phase of her development as an infant. Most psychodynamic therapists believe that the roots of manic depression are firmly planted in this time in infancy. MacKinnon and Michels (1971) compare the cycles of mania and depression to the infantile cycles of hunger and satisfaction. When the infant is hungry and is not given food right away, he fantasizes about what the gratification will be like. However, this doesn't supply the food, and eventually the fantasy gives way to stronger emotion, namely anger and depression. Manic depression works in the same way: the manic illusion of gratification is similar to the infant's illusion of obtaining food. In the end, it doesn't provide what is needed, and the cycles of anger and depression are set off.

In a deeper way, mania is a defense against depression. The client does not want to feel the loss of that which he or she loves or wants, so he or she acts in ways that hide the depression. Mania may also be a result of internal conflict in the client. MacKinnon and Michels (1971) suggest that we are observing the conflict between the defensive ego and the punitive superego. The superego makes an especially strong critique of the ego and the ego fears it will be overwhelmed. As a result, the ego defends itself through a declaration of omnipotence, claiming triumph over the superego. The client's resulting frantic activity is a flight from punishment (MacKinnon and Michels, 1971, p. 188).

Ego Psychology

The contribution of ego psychology and the study of defense mechanisms has illuminated some of the darkness surrounding manic depression. It seems that certain defenses put into action by the ego are connected to the presence of mania and depression. McWilliams (1994) identifies four defenses she has seen in her clinical work. Denial of emotional or physical distress often appears as inappropriate humor or flight from relationships. Acting out of anxious feelings often includes promiscuity, intoxication, or theft. Devaluation of significant relationships or attachments often belies a fear of loss and avoidance of depression. Omnipotent control or a similar attitude is seen in those who fear a loss of control or fear the loss of a significant other, as an effort to avoid suffering (McWilliams, 1994, p. 249).

The British psychologist Melanie Klein makes the connection between the manic defenses and the stage in infantile development she calls the depressive position. In this position the infant, for the first time, deals with the separation and loss (if only temporary) of the primary object/mother. Feelings of sadness and depression result and the child either learns to tolerate these feelings until the mother's return, or he or she copes in unhealthy ways, through the manic defenses. Klein observed that the ego used the manic defenses to counteract persecutory anxiety and depressive anxiety, and especially used the "stifling of love" (1957, p. 223) as a defense against the anxiety raised when opposite parts of the personality (such as love and hate) grow closer together. The danger that one feels from destructive impulses can produce tremendous anxiety that the manic client cannot tolerate.

Object Relations

The experience of manic depression has much to do with the object relationships of the client's past, especially with his or her parents. More specifically, the illness is a direct result of the child's loss of its parents or its traumatic separation from them. McWilliams (1994, p. 250) suggests that the client has probably had a long history of traumatic separation from significant adults in his or her life, or has at the very least a pattern of receiving criticism and emotional abuse or neglect from parents. In traditional object relations theory, the infant begins to build a relationship with his or her primary object, usually the mother who feeds the child at the breast. If the child is fed and comforted, a healthy object relationship with the mother, and eventually the father, will result. Inevitably, the needs of the child are not always met immediately and he or she becomes angry or anxious and perceives that the mother is not a loving provider but a persecuting, dangerous object. All infants will experience this. If the mother is constant in her care and comforts the angry child, he or she will eventually integrate the good mother and bad mother and go on to normal development assured by the object constancy available to him or her.

Klein, the primary proponent of object relations theory, returns to the themes of manic defense and the depressive position again and again in her work. She cites as an example the story of Orestes in Greek literature. In the tale, Orestes, the son of Agamemnon, avenges the murder of his father by killing his mother, Clytemnestra, and his mother's new husband, Aegisthus. Klein labels this an inverted Oedipus complex. She "diagnoses" Orestes with manic depression and from the story deduces that his suffering was due to persecutory anxiety and feelings of guilt that began in the depressive position of his development. Without the resolution of the conflicts of this position, he became manic depressive (Klein, 1957, p. 286).

Klein's major claims regarding manic depression include (1) a connection to the oral impulses of infancy and a "constitutional element" in manic depression, (2) a result of the loss of primary objects that are not introjected well, leading to anxiety, and (3) a link between the introjection of objects and the development of a harsh superego (Klein, 1957, pp. 78, 176, 250).

Self Psychology

Psychotherapist Laura Flanagan proposes a definition for self psychology that makes it clear for clinicians and relates this approach to the study of manic depression. She writes:

> What distinguishes self psychology is its focus on understanding the self as a cohesive whole. The emphasis is on the person's subjective sense of cohesion and well-being rather than on the supposedly objective functioning of the various aspects or parts of the self, such as the id, ego, and superego. Self psychologists try to understand the experience of self from the inside out, rather than from the outside in. (Berzoff et al., 1996, pp. 173-174)

Flanagan's co-author Joan Berzoff (Berzoff et al., 1996), joins this definition to the inner experience of manic depression. She points to "empathic failure" as a central factor in the development of manic depression. The client therefore has no healthy model for growth and therefore doesn't know how to react to the changes in life or how to tolerate the feelings of loss and anxiety. Berzoff suggests that this neglect leads to a lack of self-care and a greater vulnerability to loss. She describes the inner sensation as a "depleted self" (p. 380).

Another way of understanding the inner experience of manic depression is the sense of integration or disintegration of the self. McWilliams (1994) observes the phenomenon of fragmentation in the client who presents with manic symptoms, and the fear of "falling apart" they express (p. 250). As a way of preventing or delaying the feeling of disintegration, the manic person will function at a frenetic pace and foster a highly elated sense of mood. McWilliams also recognizes the patterns of attachment among clients with manic depression. They appear to nurture the attachment of others to themselves without any reciprocal feelings of attachment. Thus we see the manic person who is highly social, has many acquaintances, and is the life of the party, yet in their inner selves they have no significant investment in another person and experience profound loneliness.

Therapeutic Implications

The psychoanalytic literature has many methods for the treatment of manic depression. Berzoff (Berzoff et al., 1996) outlines the ways in which therapists from different traditions might approach this illness. She notes that a drive theorist might help the client get in touch with his anger. An ego psychologist might work with the client at seeing how excessive the demands of his or her superego would be and how to balance these with the needs of the ego. An object relations therapist would most likely look at any early losses the client experiences and the resulting disintegration of his ego. The self psychologist could analyze the client's previous objects (or lack thereof) and offer them a new, more dependable object in the client-therapist relationship (p. 381).

McWilliams (1994) offers some practical advice on the process of therapy with the manic-depressive client. She suggests that preventing the flight of the client from this new relationship might be the most crucial initial goal since this has been the pattern of their previous significant relationships. A second goal would be to teach the client healthy ways to end a relationship, so that good attachments can be terminated in healthy ways, with a minimum of grief. Third, medication will be needed in most cases. In addition, since the primary manic defense is denial, continual confrontation of the denial is important, in order to help the client live with the truth. Finally, McWilliams suggests that the therapy should teach the client a different way of being, one that counteracts a more manic way of behaving and relating (pp. 251-253).

In her writing on manic depression, Klein continually comes back to what it means to find healing and integration in one's life. In her essay "Envy and Gratitude" she summarizes what it might look like to achieve greater integration:

> When the infant reaches the depressive position and becomes more able to face his psychic reality, he also feels that the object's badness is largely due to his own aggressiveness and the

> ensuing projection. This insight, as we can see in the transference situation, gives rise to great mental pain and guilt when the depressive position is at its height. But it also brings about feelings of relief and hope, which in turn make it less difficult to reunite the two aspects of the object and of the self and to work through the depressive position. (Klein, 1957, p. 196)

For Klein, the conflicts of infancy determine the psychopathology of adult life. Also, the conflicts of infancy can be relived and worked through in the adult years. For the person with manic depression, healing might mean an honest look at what is on the inside, especially that which we don't want to see. Yet once it is brought to light, the client then has hope for change and integration. Reuniting the disparate parts of the self that remain divided is the key to letting go of the manic defenses that have controlled the unconscious self.

The past few decades of our inquiry into psychiatric illness have drawn from the dawning of postmodern thought, in which the value of independence prevalent a century ago has been replaced by the value of interdependence in a world that is too fragmented and isolated. The Jungian analyst Paul Kugler writes:

> In the nineteenth and early twentieth century the mind was viewed as consisting of an aggregation of separate, distinct functions, such as imagination, perception, memory, association and so on. Today this view has been replaced by a more integrated model in which "mental functions" are approached as different aspects of one homogeneous process. Even though mental behavior is a function of the entire living personality, in studying mental disorders, it continues to be useful to approach symptoms as representing disturbances in reasonably distinguishable phases of the mental process. (Kugler, 1994, p. 3)

What McWilliams might call a "different way of being" and Klein's term "integration" carry the meaning of this postmodern concept into the psychotherapeutic understanding of illness.

Alternative Approaches

Two other approaches to psychotherapy with bipolar clients fall into the cognitive-behavioral therapy category. The first belongs to

Alfred Kraus of the University of Heidelberg, whose work involves the identity issues related to mania and depression. His belief is that clients who enter therapy are struggling with an overidentification of their identity with their social role. When these are too closely connected, the client realizes he or she can never live up completely to his or her social role, and therefore feels destabilized, compulsive, and depressed. The client experiences internal conflict over the contradictory expectations of role and self. His or her ability to tolerate ambiguity is compromised and he or she suffers a breakdown of identity. This collapse can be exacerbated by a major loss, such as a change of residence or change of job and professional role.

Kraus describes the therapeutic process this way:

> The identity therapy of manic-depressives should, on the one hand, promote the development of ego-satisfying achievements; on the other, it should constantly support the possibilities of compensation (a defense in which the ego seeks another way rather than accepts disappointment) and strengthen the endangered identity structure. (Kraus, 1995, p. 200)

Kraus also reflects on the depersonalization of the self (losing a sense of one's value as a human being) in this situation, and states that therapy might involve teaching the client how to relate to his or her own self. For therapeutic approaches, he suggests reframing the client's identity issues (making an interpretation that validates his or her own experience and creates a new meaning for it), and self-reflection, particularly on life events that have proven dangerous to his or her emotional health. At the root of all this is the nature of ambiguity in the world. The client has lived to avoid ambiguity, is placed in a situation where he cannot, and must find a new way, lest he reenter the cycle of mania and depression.

Reidel et al. (2001) propose a "psychological behaviorism theory of bipolar disorder." This theory holds that multiple factors play a role in the etiology of a psychiatric illness—childhood situational factors, current situational factors, and a "basic behavioral repertoire" that interacts with situational factors. The bipolar client's repertoire includes the tendency to "grandiose self-labeling," reflecting a lack of "cautionary cognitive processes." In addition, the client has a tendency for "inappropriate arousal to psychosocial stimuli" and "maladaptive euphoria" (pp. 507-532). All of these behavioral symptoms find their etiology in the vicissitudes of original family relationships and their interaction with the child's natural predispositions. Treatment with this approach includes training clients to change negative behavior and helping them improve psychosocial conditions that might allow them to function with less internal conflict.

In both the Kraus and the Reidel models, we see connections to the theories of defense mechanisms in psychodynamic drive theory. Although these models focus on behavioral change rather than analysis, they nevertheless are both concerned with the internal conflicts and conundrums that are the stuff of traditional psychotherapy.

Transference and Countertransference

The internal experience of manic-depressive illness has been difficult for patients to describe and even more so for therapists to understand. In her book *An Unquiet Mind,* Jamison (1995) portrays eloquently the inner feelings and thoughts of the bipolar sufferer. Her writing about the subjective experience of bipolar disorder reveals both the intoxicating sensation that mania can produce, and the blackness of depression that accompanies this illness.

For the therapist working with a bipolar client, interpersonal issues can be extremely challenging. Because the manic client can be so engaging, and the depressed client so discouraging, the therapist will have many feelings elicited in the counseling office that may help the process of therapy. In his posthumously published book, *Transference and Countertransference* (1968), Racker provides much insight into the transference issues that occur with the presence of manic states in the client and analyst. This section will track what Racker has to say regarding this topic throughout his book, and how it might be helpful to the ongoing discussion in pastoral counseling regarding transference in the clinical setting. Also contributing to the dialogue will be McWilliams (*Psychoanalytic Diagnosis,* 1994). In her book she offers some practical insights into doing therapy with someone with mania and depression.

Transference and Mania

In the psychoanalytic literature mania is seen as a defensive maneuver against feelings of depression and guilt. Racker (1968) affirms this opinion and brings it into the discussion of transference and countertransference. He believed that what was happening between client and analyst reproduced conflicts from earlier in the client's childhood. When an issue arose that brought on a sense of loss and feelings of depression, the client might respond with aggressive feelings or feel that the analyst was attacking him or her. This is what can be described as a *manic defense*—an aggressive or avoidant response to an attack on the ego (p. 100).

The presence of mania in the experience of the client appears to be connected with the presence of a severe superego. The superego is the part of the unconscious mind that is the internalized parent, often correcting or scolding, sometimes judging unfairly, the actions and feelings of the client. Racker theorized that manic states were the ego's defense against an overly punitive superego (p. 115). His idea was that the internalized object, the parent, was felt as a persecutor by the client. The problem lay not with the internalization of the parental objects (those that love and accept the child) but with the child's introjection of unhealthy censure and resulting employment of the manic defense (pp. 117-118).

The bipolar client brings this internal dynamic into the therapy office. McWilliams (1994), writing from her own experience of working with manic clients, recalls:

> Manic clients can be winsome, insightful, and fascinating. They also tend to be confusing and exhausting. Once while working with a hypomanic young woman, I became aware of the fantasy that my head was in a clothes dryer, the kind in the laundromat that whirl garments in full view but too fast to track. (p. 251)

It is very likely that most therapists working with bipolar clients have had this sensation.

Racker explains how to use such countertransference reactions as information about the transference and its relationship to what has happened in the client's past that is causing distress. In the essay titled "The Countertransference Neurosis," Racker (1968) writes:

> The relation of the ego to the superego is, at bottom, a depressive and paranoid situation; the relation of the superego to the ego is, on the same plane, a manic one insofar as this term may be used to designate the dominating, controlling, and accusing attitude

> of the superego toward the ego. In this sense we may say, broadly speaking, that to a depressive, paranoid transference in the analysand, there corresponds a manic countertransference in the analyst. (p. 105)

Certainly as one ponders this dynamic the possibilities for therapy become greater. By the therapist's interpretation of this transference and the revealing of his or her own countertransference reaction, the client may see what has been troubling him or her and how it could perhaps be changed in the present.

In the essay "The Use of Countertransference," Racker (1968) reveals the process within the analyst when the manic defense is elicited. He says that

> the danger the patient fears is that he will become a helpless victim of the object's (the analyst's) sadism—of that same sadism the analyst senses in his "manic" satisfaction over dominating and defeating the bad object with which the patient was defensively identified. The perception of this manic countertransference reaction indicates what the present transference situation is and what should be interpreted. (p. 127)

Racker thus highlights the dynamics of power in the therapeutic relationship that have everything to do with the therapist's position of authority. If the therapist has feelings of domination and satisfaction, it is likely that a countertransference reaction is happening. Racker recommends interpreting it for the client and using the information in a therapeutic manner. By showing this to the client, he or she may come to understand the pattern he or she establishes in all important relationships. What the client has done with the therapist, he or she probably does with his or her parents, boss, spouse, etc. Seeing the dynamics of behavior with an authority figure, such as the therapist, allows the client to choose different ways of behaving with other such persons in his or her life.

Along these lines, Racker (1968) also looks at the unconscious processes of aggression in the analyst. The essay "The Analyst's Unconscious Mania" (p. 181) shows the link between mania and two ways in which the analyst might be feeling aggression. First would be the unconscious need for pseudoindependence, or the "denial of dependence." The other is the pseudoliberation of the instincts, or the "denial of guilt feelings." In both cases the analyst may feel anxiety and frustration in his or her work with a manic client. This anxiety will produce feelings of aggression that seek to resolve the anxiety, and the false sense of independence and freedom from guilt then arise. Racker believed that if analysts were to examine and modify these feelings of aggression, then they would not pass them on to their clients to use as manic defenses as well.

Psychoanalytic Technique and Transference

Racker (1968) has recalled for us the basic principles of transference and their application in psychotherapy. The foundational principle is "making conscious the unconscious." The corollary to this principle is "overcoming the resistances" (p. 23). Racker calls this "filling in the gaps in memory." The process involves the reexperiencing of events of one's past that have meaning for one's development. In all this work the therapist strives for "evenly-suspended attention," in which he or she is aware of his or her own feelings and can hold them in consciousness along with those of the client (p. 26). The idea here is that the analyst will notice especially his or her resistances and be able to examine them in relation to the behavior of the client. One assumes that good supervision would be a component of this process.

The primary tool of the analyst is "interpretation." This fact has never been debated in analytic circles. What has been in question is the "how" and "how often" of it. The critical factor is self-knowledge, which frees one to vary the therapeutic style in response to the individual client. Analysis is a two-way relationship, but this idea is applied in a specific way; namely, that the therapist becomes the object of the client's transference (p. 42). Once he or she can see this dynamic happening, interpret it to the client in a helpful way, and see his or her own countertransference reactions, then the therapist will have become a well-developed analyst and student of human nature. Racker even claims that the interpretations must only be about the transference dynamics, because they are the key to the way the client has related to the world in his or her life. Racker writes that "the analyst is the center of the patient's love and hate, anxiety and defense, and thus we conclude that all the patient's difficulties, all his sufferings and anxieties during the treatment, have their base in the transference" (p. 57).

Who the analyst is inside seems to be of concern to teachers of psychotherapy, and what the object relations analysts offer here is the accompanying rule to the analyst as object; that the client can be for the therapist an object as well. "The countertransference . . . is the expression of the analyst's internal constellation, stimulated by the patient who represents, for the analyst, one or another part of his ego (and id), or one or another of his objects" (p. 64). It is astounding to think that the analyst would be so involved in the process with the client, yet the point being made by Racker is that all this is unconscious process and cannot be "controlled." On the other hand, as Racker insists, the interplay of transference can be a tool for healing if attended to and used skillfully. (Racker uses the term "analyst" consistently throughout his work. In my own discussion of pastoral counseling, I hope that the counselor or therapist may make use of the same interpretations for therapeutic benefit, and not take on the process of the Freudian analyst.)

Treating Bipolar Disorder in Family Therapy

The earliest attempts at psychotherapy with entire families involved treating inpatient schizophrenics and their families all together on the psychiatric ward. Bowen came to the National Institute of Mental Health in 1954 to begin a five-year study of the interactions among families with a member who was schizophrenic (Kerr and Bowen, 1988). Bowen discovered two major patterns: first, that the families, especially mother and patient, tended to be too close, what Bowen called enmeshed; second, that the family actually played a part in perpetuating the illness in spite of themselves. It was out of these discoveries that Bowen and his colleagues applied the term *system* to the family behavior, and identified the emotional system and the relationship system.

For many who treated the severely mentally ill, these ideas gave new hope for change and new ways of treating the patients beyond medicating them. The field of family therapy was born. As with all new movements in science that gain attention, there was a time of separation and exclusivity among "purists" who practiced family therapy. Eventually, among second-generation therapists, a move toward integration with other fields of psychology began, especially psychopharmacology, psychodynamic theory, and cognitive-behavioral theory. Current research by family therapists into treating bipolar disorder finds a connection with psychoeducational treatment, notably in the work of Miklowitz and Goldstein (1997).

In their text *Bipolar Disorder: A Family-Focused Treatment Approach* the authors begin by justifying the validity of a family approach with a profoundly mentally ill person. They write:

> When recently manic patients returned from the hospital to *high-expressed-emotion* homes (those in which relatives exhibited attitudes such as criticism, hostility, or emotional overinvolvement toward the patient) or to homes characterized by negative, conflictual interactional patterns *(negative affective style)*, their chances of relapsing were much higher than if they returned to low-conflict, relatively benign home situations. Further, patients from stressful environments did not function as well over time in the social-interpersonal domain as those in less stressful environments. (p. 5)

For these doctors, changing negative patterns in the family is the primary focus, so that the patient might have a more supportive environment in which to recover from his or her illness.

Miklowitz and Goldstein offer a "family-focused treatment" process that involves six steps, as follows:

1. Assist the patient and relatives in integrating the experiences associated with episodes of bipolar disorder.
2. Assist the patient and relatives in accepting the notion of a vulnerability to future episodes.
3. Assist the patient and relatives in accepting a dependency on psychotropic medication for symptom control.
4. Assist the patient and close relatives in distinguishing between the patient's personality and his or her bipolar disorder.
5. Assist the patient and family in recognizing and learning to cope with stressful life events that trigger recurrences of bipolar disorder.
6. Assist the family in reestablishing functional relationships after the episode. (pp. 7-11)

The authors describe three phases in this type of therapy. The psychoeducation phase, in which the family learns about the nature of bipolar disorder and what to expect, comes first. The second phase is reestablishing effective communication among family members that may have deteriorated over time. The third is a problem-solving phase, in which conflict resolution is taught and practiced (pp. 12-13).

Understandably, a family in which a member has had numerous manic episodes and possibly years of untreated symptoms will probably have many wounds to heal and behaviors to change; this is a set of tasks requiring months or years of work in therapy. Yet the possibilities for helping a family change and helping the patient in that family find healing are exciting. One notes the integration of other approaches in this method. The support offered to a patient taking medications is critical for his or her compliance with medical treatment and development of the discipline to take the medications, even though they provide unpleasant side effects. Also found here is integration with behavioral therapy, in the focus on working with the family to reinforce behaviors in the patient that may prevent a recurrence of mania. Finally, we see integration with psychodynamic and psychobiological theory in the study of the origins of the illness and the uncovering of the mystery and stigma of mental illness.

Two recent studies published in the journal *Family Process* support these findings and highlight aspects of family behavior that contribute to our understanding of bipolar disorder. In a study of behavioral interaction between manic patients and their families, Rosenfarb (2001) discovered a connection between the grandiose actions of the patient and critical and nonsupportive statements of the parents. It was suggested that a circular effect is found here, and that one behavior does not *cause* the other. The author also found that an increase in this type of interaction led to a greater risk of relapse. A study by Tompson (2000, pp. 5-14) addressed the difficulty therapists have in implementing treatment for bipolar disorder. Researchers observed therapists using the psychoeducational treatment plan of Miklowitz and Goldstein to measure family affect during the course of therapy and the nature of resistance to treatment. Not surprisingly, the doctors found that the level of resistance to treatment directly matched the family's visible affect, and predicted the outcome of therapy. Affective problems in families, especially harsh and critical attitudes, mirrored the affective problems bipolar clients exhibited with the therapists. Once again we observe the integration of study here, as this theory draws upon the concept of transference as a vehicle for insight into the patterns of interaction that perpetuate the patient's illness (pp. 105-120).

In his article about structural family therapy with individuals with brain-injury trauma, Laroi (2000) makes an observation that could be applied to the family studies with bipolar patients. He writes:

> One key task of family therapy . . . is to ease the transition of the patient into his new role within the family, and facilitate adjustment to changed roles on the part of the other family members. In light of this, the importance of understanding family structure in order to plan and implement psychological treatment seems particularly important. . . . Structural family therapy postulates that transactional patterns depend on the way people experience reality. Therefore, to change the way the family members look at reality requires the development of new ways of interacting in the family. (p. 72)

Laroi is thinking about brain-injured individuals and applying family therapy principles to their treatment. He offers those who treat bipolar disorder an insight into the roles played by family members and how they may change when bipolar illness appears. The manic patient will no longer carry out his or her role in the family, or he or she will have a role that the family assigns him or her because of the illness. This changes when the patient undergoes successful treatment.

A final variation on family therapy approaches comes from the narrative school of family psychology. In her article titled "Relational Narratives of the Self," Fishbane (2001) reflects on the view of the self in Western culture and how it is changing to our benefit. The primary view of the self in psychology has been an individual self, apart from its relationships with others. In fact, the autonomous self has been used in the psychodynamic literature as the locus of treatment and definition of health and integration. Fishbane notes the gradual shift over the past two decades to a more relational view of the self in the family therapy literature. She cites the work of Ivan Boszormenyi-Nagy and the contextual school as giving new life to the idea of storytelling and mythmaking in psychotherapy. What became clear was the necessity for clients to tell their stories and define themselves in terms of their stories and relationships.

The concept of interdependence is central to this therapeutic approach. It describes the way in which a person who comes for therapy may find a remedy for the isolation and separation they feel. Fishbane's work focuses on the experiences of women, yet applies to those of men as well—especially to the lives of those with psychiatric illness. When the symptoms of bipolar disorder or schizophrenia have isolated sufferers from their communities of support, their definition of self is changed. No longer are they "selves-in-relation" but persons cut off from the families and friends that define who they are. The author points to the work of social constructionists as important to this idea. "Rather than locating identity and meaning-making within the mind of the individual, they see identity as socially-constructed: We live in and through the narrative identities that we develop in conversation with one another" (p. 275). In contrast to this are traditional views of self: "The narrative of the separate self valorizes independence and emphasizes boundaries as self-protective mechanisms. By contrast, the narrative of the relational self emphasizes authenticity and voice in relationship, and sees boundaries as points of meeting or communicating" (p. 275).

The implications for family psychotherapy are tremendous. When the therapist brings the relational view of self to the treatment room, he or she recognizes the importance of all family relationships to the patient's life and well-being, including multigenerational connections. For clients who have bipolar illness, change will be necessary both in themselves and in the family. In the relational-narrative model, these changes happen together. "Change in therapy is a relational process" (Fisbane, 2001, p. 277). Attention is paid to the life cycle of the whole family, including where each member is in his or her individual journey and how each individual's story fits into their story as a group. Respect is given to the client's story and the family's as well, and this mutual respect is developed as a relational skill in the work of therapy.

Fishbane concludes her article with a discussion of connection and disconnection in close relationships. Families who have a mentally ill member know firsthand the experience of disconnection that is felt among the patient and other family members. "In a relational model of psychological development, disconnection from others is viewed as one of the primary sources of human suffering" (p. 280). The question arises of why one would fear connection with those they love. "In our deep desire to make connection, we keep large parts of ourselves out of connection. The fear is that if one brought oneself fully into relationship, including hidden or shameful parts, one would lose the connection with the other" (p. 280).

It is difficult for family members to understand what their loved ones are experiencing internally. It is equally difficult to understand their behavior. As a result, a seemingly unresolvable disconnection is created. The client cannot risk being completely honest, and the family cannot bear the pain. For healing to occur, Fishbane suggests the creation of a story that includes the honest portrayal of the illness and that tells of reconnection and hope (pp. 273-291).

Chapter 2

Current Pastoral Counseling Theory

CASE STUDY

Marianne has been my client over the past year. She is a twenty-five-year-old woman who came to the counseling center with increasing panic attacks and anxiety. The most recent episode before she came in for counseling involved an experience in a bar: someone had playfully pulled her ponytail, and she had a panic attack and ran out. This experience jarred memories of physical and sexual abuse by an older stepbrother, which occurred when she was a teenager.

Marianne seemed to be a friendly, funny, and intelligent woman. She was living at home with her mother, stepfather, and brother, who was fourteen years old. She was employed full-time as a home health aide. She was extremely overweight and dressed in very dark clothing. She had a two-year relationship with her boyfriend, Tim, who was a musician. Her home situation was sometimes stressful, and included a great deal of conflict with her mother. Her stepfather had been a true father to her, and was generally kind, but not very available. The stepbrother who abused her was no longer living in the area. Her biological father was no longer around, and his whereabouts were unknown. She described her fourteen-year-old brother as having a "rage disorder."

Some of Marianne's symptoms included those of posttraumatic stress disorder (PTSD), including nightmares, recurring flashbacks to the abuse, fear of social situations and all men, anxiety attacks, drug use (mainly marijuana), and sexual dysfunction. She reported that she and Tim had an occasional sexual encounter but she is unable to achieve orgasm. She also exhibited signs of bipolar disorder, most notably regular cycles of depression and mania. Her depression seemed to occur more often, probably five to six times per year, and manic phases less often, sometimes just once per year. For her, the mania was marked by sleeplessness and chaotic thoughts, and attempts at self-medication through drug use.

I was amazed that Marianne could work on any of these issues with a male therapist, but she seemed to be able to talk frankly about everything and was not visibly afraid of me. I realize that I may be quite different from most of the men in her life, or may even be more like her boyfriend, Tim. It

The Treatment of Bipolar Disorder in Pastoral Counseling

doi:10.1300/5696_03

seemed to be critical for Marianne to tell her story and be heard. She didn't really have anyone in whom she could confide her most troubling thoughts and feelings (even Tim). She didn't seem to understand the nature of her trauma and what a normal reaction might be. We used the book *Courage to Heal* (Bass and Davis, 1994) to help with this.

It became very important to explore and uncover her family dynamics, especially the keeping of secrets regarding the trauma and her mother's cooperation in it. I got the sense that Marianne just wanted to scream out and tell the world what an asshole her stepbrother was. She wasn't able to scream in our sessions and the only emotions she could vent were some tears.

Marianne wanted more safe social interaction (connectedness). She also had a desire to go back to college. She had many gifts and talents, especially people skills and artistic and musical gifts. In therapy she worked to define her hopes and dreams, and began to act on them. She recognized a gift she had for reaching out to the "outsider" and including those who might otherwise be excluded (community).

In our sessions, Marianne would often speak of a girlfriend, Tracey, with whom she would spend a lot of time. I always got the feeling there was more to their relationship than friendship, and after we had been in therapy for a few months, Marianne confided that she had romantic feelings for Tracey. This was difficult for her because she was working on her relationship with her boyfriend and now she feared that she might be bisexual. She wondered if this had anything to do with her sexual trauma or whether it was simply her nature.

Marianne was in therapy for one year. She worked hard. Sometimes she sabotaged treatment through missed appointments and coming to appointments "stoned," but mostly she was a delight to work with. I believe her accomplishments were as follows: She was able to tell her story, usually in pieces as she recalled the details, she verbalized her pain and fear openly, she began to establish herself as a confident and capable person, and she achieved better self-esteem. She uncovered family dynamics that are harmful and learned to be more assertive with her boyfriend and tell him what she needed. She identified some dreams for the future, especially her plans to become a chiropractor, and she discovered her spiritual resources for personal growth and inner peace, especially the ideas of synchronicity (all things working together for good) and of treasuring silence.

BEGINNINGS

> The most significant direct contribution of clergymen to mental health is their counseling and shepherding of troubled persons.
>
> Clinebell, 1977, p. 1

Can pastoral counselors contribute to the treatment of those who have major psychiatric disorders? Can pastoral counseling offer a unique approach to helping the mentally ill in their process of recovery? From its very beginnings, the field of pastoral counseling has placed itself at the center of care for those with depression, anxiety, grief, and more severe pathology such as manic depression. The founders of this movement wrote eloquently about their hopes for how pastoral counselors might take part in the dialogue of mental health providers. One of the early voices was that of Howard Clinebell.

In *The Mental Health Ministry of the Local Church* (1972) Clinebell suggested two levels at which religious professionals could help the mentally ill. First were the opportunities for "informal counseling" available to the pastor at the church and on pastoral visits. He writes:

> Pastoral care is the multifaceted ministry of caring for the spiritual welfare and growth of persons of all ages. This function is invaluable as a sustaining, nurturing influence in the lives of millions of people. The minister's caring symbolizes the caring of the religious community and of God and is expressed in many ways . . . this supportive ministry is indispensable to the maintenance of robust mental health. (p. 212)

The author is clearly seeking to connect the ministry of counseling to the community of faith, and measures its value in the establishment of connection between the counselee and the body of Christ. Healing and wholeness happen not in isolation but in the nurturing community of the church.

Second, Clinebell sees formal pastoral counseling as similar to secular psychotherapy, but also identifies ways in which pastoral counseling is unique among the mental health professions. The pastoral counselor is trained in theology and philosophy as well as psychology, and is equipped to create, as Tillich put it, the "helping encounter in the ultimate dimension" (Tillich, 1956). The pastoral counselor offers the client a perspective from which wholeness in the human personality is understood as taking place in the context of a relationship with God. The major theological themes—"guilt, grace, sin, alienation, meaninglessness, death and rebirth"—are thus open to discussion in the pastoral counseling setting. In addition, the pastoral counselor, in his role as religious authority, can help clients explore themes of relationships with authority figures (parents, God) in the transference. Finally, the pastoral counselor has available to him or her the elements of pastoral practice, Scripture, prayer, and the Sacraments. Used with sensitivity to the client's beliefs and background, these can be powerful sources of reconciliation with God and spiritual wholeness.

Clinebell offers a number of types of counseling available to the pastor, and suggests that he or she be versed in more than one of these approaches to therapy. Marriage and family counseling views personal problems in the context of the family. The family is seen as an "interpersonal organism" in which healing will occur in the reestablishing of open patterns of communication and awareness of roles and behavior. Supportive growth-action counseling focuses on the establishment of a reliable relationship with the pastor, in the context of which the clients are enabled to make decisions and handle the stresses of life. The need for referral counseling stems from the fact that troubled people tend to seek their pastor's guidance first before exploring mental health resources in the community. Good referral counseling by the pastor can help the parishioner not only find the appropriate specialized help they need (especially psychiatric care) but remove any roadblocks to seeking this kind of care. Finally, religious-existential problem counseling can help the client sort out spiritual problems from psychosis. Clinebell recognizes the difficulty of distinguishing between the two, yet upholds the importance of attending carefully to both. In maintaining this dual focus, pastoral counselors offer clients something unique among mental health professionals.

Seward Hiltner was another voice in the early pastoral care and counseling movement. He saw pastors as advocates for the mentally ill in obtaining mental health services in the community (Hiltner, 1975, pp. 965-970). He remembered the pioneering work of Dorothea Dix in the nineteenth century in lobbying state governments for more humane care in state institutions. He recognized Clifford Beers, a former psychiatric patient who went on to found the national advocacy group now known as the National Mental Health Association. He also learned from William and Karl Menninger, who worked to reform the conditions in Kansas psychiatric hospitals and created better environments for inpatients and ways they could be discharged and live in their communities again.

Hiltner spoke of the responsibility of society to treat the mentally ill and the power that pastors have in their communities to effect change. In his book *Theological Dynamics* (1972) Hiltner reflected on a metaphor for the church that applies ". . . the leaven that works in the bread or the fire that needs to burn when there is rigidity or stagnation" (p. 119). The author sees the church as having a special mission to the community at large as a voice that calls for social change. As leaders in their communities of faith, pastors exercise power on behalf of the church to witness for the care of the forgotten in society, such as the mentally ill.

John Patton has been an engaging voice in the evolution of pastoral counseling from its beginnings. His article "Pastoral Counseling Comes of Age" (1981) offers some ways in which this profession can find its identity in a changing environment. First, the territory among counselors of all methods and schools is a shared one, but pastoral counseling has a unique view of healing: "The pastoral counselor offers an identifiable witness to Christian meanings and commitments and their relevance for health care" (p. 230). Patton describes this as a visible witness in the world that calls all of us to a view of the "religious dimension in life."

Second, pastoral counseling must develop an "appropriate norm" or methodology for its work. Patton suggests "relational humanness" as a way of envisioning pastoral counseling.

> Relational humanness has revealed God's humanness for us in Jesus Christ. God's relation to the world through a person strongly suggests that the clue for development of personal meaning in life rests in the quality of relationships and the character of humanness revealed therein. (p. 230)

The counseling relationship, once thought to be about the intrapsychic world only, now has everything to do with the relationship in the counseling office and out in the client's world.

Third, Patton argues for the pastoral counseling ministry as an "extension of the church." It has been to the detriment of all pastoral work that counselors have not had "accountability" to their denominations. He writes that what clients receive at a pastoral counseling center "is not primarily treatment for depression but a significant relationship and an interpretation of life that is intended to break through their limited way of perceiving the human situation" (p. 231).

Patton believes that this kind of accountability and connection to the church is even created within the center itself: "It is a community of ministers, both ordained and lay, who work together in order to correct and learn from each other's theory and practice of the faith" (p. 231). The emphasis here in Patton's writing is on the presence of community in the treatment of clients. That community can be a resource or can be ignored, but will always be there because of God's communing with us in Christ. If true healing is to take place, whether for couples with marital problems or individuals with bipolar disorder, it must take place within the community of faith, where God is at work in the Holy Spirit (pp. 229-231).

Rodney Hunter, professor emeritus of pastoral theology at Candler School of Theology, takes up the concerns expressed by Patton. In his article, "Spiritual Counsel: An Art in Transition" (2001), Hunter looks at the problems and advantages posed by the practice of pastoral counseling within the community of faith. As ideal as this mode of practice sounds, problems exist. These concern the financial survival of this enterprise, balanced with the needs of clients for a loving community. Our concepts of for-profit health care institutions and counseling practices seem at odds with a church-based model that stresses ministry and mission:

> Missing in much contemporary discussion of pastoral care is the structural element that makes community dependable and trustworthy over time. Terms like institution and organization suggest what's missing, for these are vitally important for providing the secure boundaries and resources necessary for trustworthy, deep, enduring relationships and for a stable community that encourages healthy and meaningful personal living. (Hunter, 2001, p. 20)

In spite of his concern for the nature of faith communities as healing places and the place of pastoral counselors within those communities, Hunter places the future survival of pastoral counseling in the local churches: "Perhaps pastoral counseling will reaffirm its pastoral identity through a closer institutional tie to the churches and community organizations, and will develop forms of economic support that are relatively independent of managed care and insurance reimbursement" (p. 24). Certainly the financial realities of surviving in the "business" of pastoral counseling are severe, yet wherever there are pastors and churches and hurting people, there will be pastoral counseling. As Hunter says and this book affirms, the location of pastoral counseling in the community of faith is vital for the healing of a person as an interdependent member of a loving group of believers.

PASTORAL COUNSELING WITH THE BIPOLAR CLIENT

For the person with bipolar disorder, the reality of medication is unavoidable. The severity of manic episodes coupled with the depths of depression, and the availability of medications to manage these symptoms, make it likely that bipolar clients who come for pastoral counseling will already be on mood stabilizers, antidepressants, and/or antipsychotics. If not, then the pastoral counselor should explore the possibility of referral to a psychiatrist for diagnosis and treatment. The relief available through drug treatment is too efficacious to resist in favor of a longer-term and less-promising psychotherapy. On the other hand, medications will only address the symptoms of mania and depression; the bipolar sufferer will still require counseling for the long-term effects of the illness and the changes necessary for recovery.

Ashbrook (1994) offers helpful insight into what the cooperation between psychiatrist and pastoral counselor might look like on behalf of the bipolar client. In his article "Psychopharmacology and Pastoral Counseling: Medication and Meaning" he recognizes enormous change in the fields of psychiatry and pastoral counseling in the past few decades. He calls these the "remedicalization of psychiatry" and the "retheologizing of pastoral therapy." New drug therapies have appeared at faster and faster rates, offering psychiatrists new tools for treating illnesses that were once hopeless. During the same time period pastoral counseling has been engaged in forming its identity vis-à-vis secular psychotherapy and in reintegrating religious themes and "meaning-making" processes. Yet it is becoming more and more apparent that mind and body are interdependent, and that interdisciplinary cooperation is necessary.

> In the best of all possible situations, psychiatrist and pastoral therapist collaborate on behalf of the patient's or client's need. Increasing evidence supports a positive impact of medication in

> many genetically based disorders. The evidence also suggests the desirability, even the necessity, of talk-oriented therapy utilizing the transferential dynamics of the therapeutic relationship to return the person to a growth-emerging story. (Ashbrook, 1994, p. 17)

What is that "growth-emerging" story for Ashbrook? He describes it quite simply in a case report of a bipolar client he once treated. Her illness caused very exaggerated mood swings and every part of her life "seemed to excite or fragment her." They decided to pursue a concurrent therapy of medication and psychotherapy. She described relief from many of her symptoms after a few weeks. The client succeeded by "learning how to handle the ups and down of living" (p. 8). Although this is not a terribly dramatic case, it represents a most common one: a functional person who finds life more and more compromised by psychiatric illness, which he or she may not even be able to identify. The therapist listens to the person's story and makes an appropriate referral for medication, continuing to see him or her in supportive therapy.

Ashbrook explores the cooperative treatment that can be offered to clients with mania and depression. His idea is that the pastoral counselor works in the area of meaning when an illness disables someone. A different case study illustrates what Ashbrook means. In his work with another person, the client resisted the use of medication, preferring the weekly counseling instead. "Meaning" in this setting was important to both the client and the therapist in many ways. First, the creation of a trusting environment gave the client's chaotic life more order and helped her to find meaning in the struggles of her past. Second, teaching the client about the effects of chemical imbalances on feelings and behavior helped the client understand her previous experience of depression. Ashbrook concludes the discussion with this observation:

> Drugs can take the edge off the intensity of pain, yet dialogue is necessary to reestablish a trusting relationship in an ambiguous world. . . . Religious faith provides a way of assessing a shift from an externally oriented victimization of the client, as in identifying with Jesus on the cross, to an internally anchored sense of Christ participating with one in her or his suffering. (p. 17)

What Ashbrook has done here for pastoral counselors is establish the boundaries of our work with clients, while at the same time contextualizing therapy in the overall care. In the case of Marianne, a clear need for psychotherapy and medication existed, given the severity of her symptoms and personal history. Yet as therapist and client, we had to move gradually from a shared understanding of her experience, through the adaptations she had made through self-medication and compensating behavior, to a new way of coping that included healthy self-exploration and prescription medication under a doctor's care. Spiritually, Marianne had to define what it was she believed, find within those beliefs a connection to her suffering, and apply to her life the comfort available through her faith.

Savage (2001) makes another connection between secular psychotherapy and pastoral counseling in his study of Alfred Adler's depth psychology. The author writes that Adler valued the religious beliefs of his clients and sought to incorporate Christian themes in his theory and practice. "Adler believed that the ultimate purpose of psychotherapy was to improve the human social condition" (p. 1). This became more fully developed in Adler's theory of community feeling, which saw the highest value placed on the sense of belonging to the community and being accepted by the community. As Savage describes it, Adler's ideas are beneficial to the client with psychiatric illness who may be isolated from community or self. Two such applications might be these:

> Individuated psychology is in need of a deep eternal Self, as well as broad social concerns. The deep eternal self and its broad social concerns finds a home in the Christian community. . . . and the Christian life style which seeks health and seeks to prevent illness (physical and spiritual) is lived out in community. (pp. 3-4)

Savage is talking about reconciling the vertical nature of the client's relationship with God and self, and the horizontal nature of the client's life in the community. A theory of psychology that incorporates both dimensions is better for clients and addresses their needs more fully. Savage, who is a hospital chaplain, finds Adler's theory valuable for his own ministry to people in the hospital setting. Helping the patient find healing and hope through community is a high priority for the pastor in this environment.

In tandem with Adler's views of psychotherapy and pastoral theology comes the model developed by Lacan (1964) on the fundamental concepts of psychoanalysis. His concepts are actually theological themes that arise in therapy that are available to the therapist to use on the client's behalf in growth and change. The most intriguing of these concepts is the dual idea of redemption and Sabbath. As Lupton (2000) describes in her article about Lacan's theory, Sabbath

> proffers an opportunity to traverse *nihilo* (the sense of nothingness or meaninglessness) to reconfigure and repunctuate *nihilo* the signifying sequence of the week, breaking up the endless repetition of the day-to-day with the possibility of rest that embraces the created and social worlds, extending to (all). In the weekly redemption opened up by the Sabbath, the *nihil* at the heart of creation *ex nihilo* is separated out from the orders it constellates. (p. 2)

The idea of the Sabbath as being redemptive, as addressing the "nothingness" of despair, has great value for pastoral counseling with the mentally ill. The promise of rest for someone with a troubled and chaotic mind is in itself redemptive, as there has been no hope until now. Furthermore, the redemption of a life that had no promise of wholeness is something that can only be fully interpreted by the religious professional in his or her priestly role. This can be the unique role of pastoral counseling.

TREATMENT MODELS

In order to treat clients for major mood disorders, one must have a clear conception of the disorder and a concrete method for implementation. Meier (1997) offers such a model in an article on the treatment of major depression. He gives a unique, pastoral conception of the disorder and the response by the pastoral counselor

> . . . to include the importance of inauthentic living with self, God, and others and the failure to strive for wholeness. . . . Striving for spiritual wholeness and authentic living becomes the

> pivotal experience which serves to integrate one's thinking processes and set of assumptions, one's affective and emotional responses, and one's wishes, yearnings and needs. (p. 7)

In short, Meier argues that a healing in the person's spirit effects changes in his or her entire psychological being. The therapist, in treating the depressed client, helps him or her to find more authentic ways of living that honors his or her uniqueness as human being.

The method employed here is a two-part method that Meier describes as "self-discovery and action oriented and interdisciplinary in nature" (p. 9). The author's ideas resemble cognitive-behavioral theory, with its emphasis on recognizing and changing dysfunctional behavior and becoming aware of negative and self-defeating thinking. Also, Meier credits the traditional pastoral counseling heritage in the work of Carl Rogers, and places its assumptions about the character of the therapist in the "three Rogerian core conditions, namely, empathy, unconditional positive regard and congruence" (p. 8). He believes that the pastoral counselor must move beyond this as a method for therapy yet depend on the guidance of Rogers' ideas as the fundamentals of good counseling.

Another useful part of Meier's research is the discovery of certain "constituents" of depression, which he found as feeling obligated, loss of personal space, sense of powerlessness, unexpressed feelings of anger, feelings of guilt, and the desire to become empowered for action. Each of these characteristics points to the client's experience of incongruence with the outside world, and to the need to change negative thinking and learn new behaviors that foster congruence. In each of these areas Meier makes connection to the various dimensions of the client's life, one of which is the church community. Transference was noted between the client's relationships in the church and relationships with parents. The outcome of examining this dynamic was to see the transference with God. Meier observes that, in recovery, clients

> related to God more as a friend than as a demanding and critical judge, accepted anger as a legitimate human experience, became more relaxed and content, lived more in the here and now, let go of those things over which he had no control, and lived according to what he believed was right for him. (p. 25)

Once again, the locus of healing and wholeness became the community of faith, albeit a transferential locus. With the guidance of an alert therapist, the transference could be noted and the depression relieved.

The principles of systems theory have found a home in pastoral counseling practice. One of the eloquent voices for this application is Larry Kent Graham of the Iliff School of Theology. In his article "From Psyche to System" (1992) he gives treatment guidelines that incorporate both systems theory and theological meaning. The five principles he outlines are organicity, simultaneity, conscientization, advocacy, and adventure. Organicity is the reciprocal connectedness we experience with others, in which the system becomes more or less stable. Simultaneity is the concept that changes in one part of the system can bring change in another part. Conscientization occurs when the pastoral counselor helps the client to see the impact of their actions on the greater social order and make choices in light of this awareness. Advocacy happens when the pastoral caregiver helps to shape public policy through his or her influence and that of the faith communities he or she represents. Adventure, as Graham says, is when "God is present as an ally on the side of transformation and liberative change, and that such change is an expected but unpredictable gift of grace and fruit of hope." The author calls counselors and clients "adventurers of the spirit" (p. 332).

Graham brings the ideas of systems theory into the pastoral realm and makes a strong case for using family therapy in pastoral counseling. What he suggests may transfer to therapy with bipolar clients. As has been shown, the effects of this illness on the families of the sufferers and the opportunities for change within families that will help the client find some peace are promising. The bipolar person has the capacity for working through his social environment and finding healing in his relationships. Graham suggests that it is the give-and-take of individual change and the process of therapy that fosters continuous change.

Another school of therapeutic thought that has found a place in pastoral counseling is narrative therapy. In this way of helping, the client and therapist work together at telling the story of the client's illness in the context of his or her entire experience of life, in order to construct an alternative, more empowering story. Narrative therapists see their method more as structure than technique. Each counseling relationship is unique in that what the client brings is his or her own story. The therapist collaborates with the client in the building of the story as a "co-narrator" (Monteleone, 1997, pp. 1-3).

In his article for the *Journal of Pastoral Counseling,* Robert Monteleone (1999) proposed a model for treating clients with depression. This model, called "voice, support, and strategy" brings the narrative method into the pastoral counseling office in service of those with severe psychiatric disturbance. In this three-part model, the therapist first works with the client to find his or her voice, that is, to express the client's own unique point of view and to fight back against the muting effect of depression. The second task is establishing support, by finding resources in the client's community that will be places of unconditional love and care. The third task is to develop strategies for dealing with depression.

In his clinical practice, Monteleone has found that narrative approaches to therapy work well with depression and other psychiatric disturbances. The author stresses the necessity for telling the story without an immediate attempt to solve the problem: "In an effort to reach conclusions, so much of the complexity and uniqueness of a person or situation is lost. A narrative does not seek conclusions but only markers in which to navigate" (p. 1).

In this description of narrative therapy with the mentally ill, one sees the value of helping the client develop the story, for one day that person will leave therapy and go on to create the rest of the story of his or her life. Finding "markers" along the way will help the client negotiate a rocky path when the therapist is no longer present.

> So we tune into the inner circle of events with a sense of wonderment, resisting the temptation of labeling or reducing storytellers' life events and facts into some neat, tidy theory that might readily explain their behavior, or worse yet, their lives. (Monteleone, 1997, p. 2)

What may most help the client in therapy is the "cocreating" that goes on in the storytelling. The processes in that person's family system have made them in part who they are and who they will be in the future. Understanding the story of their "creation" may lead the way to redemption.

CONFLICT IN PASTORAL COUNSELING

Some pastoral theologians have become interested in scientific study of the biological beginnings of psychiatric disturbance and how theologians and pastors might join in the exploration. The logical place to begin was the brain, and the one theologian who could enter the fray was Ashbrook, in a book co-authored with Albright titled *The Humanizing Brain: Where Religion and Neuroscience Meet* (1998). Ashbrook had already been exploring the theory of the two hemispheres of the brain and how that might inform pastoral theology. What he and Albright propose is an evolutionary understanding of the brain in three parts, reflecting the functions and behaviors in each part. The following helps to explain the schema:

Evolutionary Stage	Function	Experience of God
reptilian	autonomic regulation	jealousy of God
mammalian	emotions, memory	nurturing God
neocortex	language, reasoning	metaphors of God

Can any of this be of help in developing an understanding of the illnesses of the brain and can theology be a resource in treating mental illnesses? What is most helpful is bringing together spheres of thought once deemed irreconcilable. The dual notions of body and mind, reason and emotion, and theology and medicine had been separate since the days of the Enlightenment. Ashbrook and Albright help reconnect these modes of thought in a way that may shed more light on the nondual nature of illness.

In his review, Peterson (1999) points to the more subtle intent of this book and of Ashbrook and Albright's work in general:

> Ashbrook and Albright argue that a central feature of human cognition is our predisposition to humanize what we perceive. This humanizing begins with the self. In the past two decades, the growing trend in both neuroscience and philosophy has been to counter the old reductionist tradition that we are nothing but a collection of neurons, nothing but the physical constituents of our bodies. Rather, our selves emerge from all the activities of those buzzing neurons. Avoiding the extremes of both a material-

> istic *monism* and a mind-body *dualism*, Ashbrook and Albright advocate an emergent *holism* that recognizes that the brain has a "bottom up" influence on the mind, but also that the mind has a "topdown" influence on the brain. (pp. 84-88)

Clinicians who treat persons with mental illnesses know firsthand the complexity of their clients' experience. To lump all their feelings and thoughts into a reductionist theory does them an injustice. To appreciate the staggeringly complex nature of their illness and to use that understanding to build a treatment plan can only improve clients' chances at a measure of wholeness in all spheres of existence.

Evangelical theologians have been skeptical regarding the content of these explorations into mind and body, and offer warnings about biological treatment of mental disorders. In their article "The Gospel According to Prozac" Barshinger et al. (1995) look at some anecdotal material of people who have been treated for depression with Prozac and other SSRIs. Their research affirms the efficacy of such drugs and applauds the efforts to treat severe psychiatric disturbance. Their questions remain:

> Are Prozac and similar antidepressants potentially a shortcut for people to feel good without the character-forming discipline of faith and religious belief?
>
> What is sin and what is biology? Can a pill do what the Holy Spirit or human will could not? (p. 34)

Each of these questions helps to make clear what evangelical theology brings to the discussion—namely, the reality of human nature as a broken and divided experience, including the self, and the need for a redeemer to restore the brokenness. The crux of the debate here is the locus of human brokenness and the capacity of individual faith to heal it. Inherent in these questions is an individual orientation to faith and a dualist understanding of the human person.

Nevertheless, the authors come back to the heart of their own anxiety, which is a perceived threat against Christianity by medicine. They respond with a rational and practical claim that will help evangelical believers decide about receiving drug treatment:

> So, will Prozac replace religion? If religion is only to make people happy, then Prozac can replace religion. But if religion is to bring people into contact with ultimate reality, then Prozac cannot. Happiness is a bonus, not the end goal. (Barshinger et al., 1995, p. 37)

A variation on the theme of religion and science is religion and psychology. These two disciplines have been in conversation for many decades in the pastoral care movement in this country. Moderate and liberal theologians have embraced the insights of psychology as informative in constructing a theological anthropology. Even evangelical seminaries have departments of pastoral counseling and psychology that train ordained pastors to use the methods of psychology in service to the church. Yet there have been cautionary voices in this dialogue, notably William Kilpatrick of Boston College and Stanton Jones of Wheaton College.

In an article titled "Faith and Therapy," Kilpatrick argues for firm separation of the Christian faith and secular psychotherapy, even where the two are practiced side by side. He suggests the following dangers of mixing them: a diminished sense of sin, a diminished sense of the sacred, no room for the concept of transcendence, and a greater focus on the self and its material and psychological needs. In a more defensive posture, the author writes of the "attacks" by psychotherapy on Christian culture:

> If this is difficult to see, it is because of the fog that the culture of therapy emits—an empathic fog which surrounds us and confuses us and prevents us from seeing life clearly. We wander around in this fog thinking our enemy is our friend because he is so exquisitely concerned with our health. (Kilpatrick, 1999, p. 26)

Given Kilpatrick's position on the eroding importance of Christian faith in culture, one can appreciate his concern for the elevation of psychotherapy to the status of religion in our society. Nevertheless, his point is overstated in that the psychotherapeutic establishment is not involved in an organized takeover of the Christian Church. One idea that seemed to address the dialogue between science and religion is the concept of transcendence and the experience of this in the believer. He remarks that contemporary Catholics have lost their understanding of the doctrine of the Real Presence of Christ in the Sacraments. Nevertheless, believers of all faiths and all places celebrate communion in much the same way and experience very powerfully the presence of the Risen Christ among them. For members of our parishes who cannot be reached by God any other way, communion is that one, visible sign that Christ walks the way of suffering with them.

Jones' writing has often been in response to secular psychologists and evolutionary psychologists in particular. In his article "My Genes Made Me Do It" (1995) Jones reviews a book on evolutionary psychology and takes up the larger issue of the biological nature of human behavior. It is his contention that Christians can accept the scientific discoveries of the brain and have room within theology for God as creator of human biological nature. His concern is for the one-sided view of humanity as driven by the desire for procreation.

> We are sexual, but we are not merely sexual. We are biological, but not merely biological. We were created for more than that—we were created first for a loving and intimate relationship with our Creator, and also for loving connectedness with spouse, children, family, friends, and neighbors, with our brothers and sisters in Christ and with people of a hurting world who do not know Christ, and for meaningful work in a real world as responsible stewards over the created order. (p. 18)

Jones builds another bridge across the chasm of evolutionary chaos when he raises the theme of connectedness as biological. An overarching theme of this book is connectedness, and the idea that it is part of our very nature to be linked to others in the living of life. Although Jones rejects the theory of evolution, he places himself squarely in the midst of those scientists and theologians who see our native connection to other human beings and all of nature. This connectedness is the crucible of health.

THE RELIGIOUS EXPERIENCE OF SUFFERING

Many attempts have been made to quantify or secularize the experience of spiritual suffering in the believer. More helpful have been theories that understand both the temporal and the spiritual in the realm of human distress. O'Connor (2002, pp. 137-148) explores the experience of the mystic John of the Cross and his description of the "dark night of the soul." The thesis is that John was suffering depression, and the similarities in John's writing to the criteria by which depression is diagnosed are inescapable. The dark night comes when the practices that once brought the believer close to God are no longer sufficient, and the feeling of "dryness" or "emptiness" in one's spirit invades. One may feel completely alienated from God where before there was intimacy and comfort. So it is in the experience of depression, where feelings of hopelessness and emptiness flood in, along with low energy, low self-esteem, low appetite, and insomnia/hypersomnia. The author even includes the analysis of the psychiatrist G. G. May (1982), who commented on the link between these two experiences: "If the frustration in prayer is neither surrendered nor experienced as anger, it may be turned against oneself and breed true depression" (p. 85).

O'Connor mentions the two pathways of religious experience, the cataphatic and the apophatic, and highlights John's experience as the apophatic, or via negativa. He writes that in this tradition

> no images, ideologies, or cultural expressions can adequately convey all that God is, and revelation brings one into mystery characterized by emptiness, dryness and the absence of the sense of God's presence. Two classic Western expressions of this tradition include the Carmalite (silent) experience and the silence of Quaker meetings. (p. 137)

This will be further explored in Chapter 3 as the Quaker approach to health and wholeness is reviewed and offered as a way to healing from manic depression.

The phenomenon of demonic possession demands the attention of any study of religion and science, and religion and health. The stories of the New Testament portray the struggle between Jesus and the forces of death. Capps (2001) interprets the story of the exorcism of the demon-possessed boy in Mark 9:14-29. He offers both a scientific/psychoanalytic opinion and a theological diagnosis that illumine the occurrence of demon possession.

The biological process is seizure disorder or epilepsy. The psychoanalytic component, as Freud described in his work on demonology, was the presence of repressed neuroses that issued in psychotic symptoms, including self-destructive behavior. Capps also proposes the father-son relationship as a source of conflict for the boy, who is raised in a society that would inflict suffering on the child to strengthen him. The child's behavior is in part the rebellious, angry lashing out at a world that hurts and frustrates him. The theological diagnosis includes the assigning of an unknown cause to evil spirits, but also the power of the redemptive Jesus and his attention to those with psychological distress, especially young people (pp. 135-147).

Capps further sees the story as a means for Jesus to be with those at the margins of society—the mentally ill. In fact, Jesus is portrayed as the true father in the story, reaching down to the boy and lifting him up after the exorcism. Jesus as Father carries archetypal meaning, but here it is contextual—Jesus shows what a true father would do for a troubled son.

A final study of the nature of religious suffering has to do with guilt. This uniquely human experience is often where discussions of religion and psychology come together, as in the conversation of Paul Tillich and James Ashbrook (1988) published as *Paul Tillich in Conversation*. Tillich clarifies the difference in meaning between the guilt feelings one has when one has done wrong, and the state of guilt in which we all are as human beings, by our estrangement from God. Again he relates the difference and the true meaning of forgiveness in terms of Pauline theology:

> Forgiveness is only the more vivid description of the more abstract term "being justified by grace through faith." Faith is receiving forgiveness; grace is the divine giving of forgiveness. The whole act is in a Paulinian terminology, which was Rabbinic terminology, called justification. (p. 53)

Tillich further clarifies his idea of "ultimate forgiveness" by remembering the story of the two criminals on the cross next to Jesus:

> For instance, one of the two criminals crucified with Jesus is accepted. This does not mean that he is not a criminal. He is guilty. But his guilt is taken up as forgiveness, something which shall not be valid in the relationship of God and himself, as it is not valid in the relationship when we forgive each other. (p. 54)

This notion of the recognition of guilt and divine grace in spite of it are critical to wholeness.

What, then, is the relationship between guilt and mental health? In an article titled "Religion, Guilt and Mental Health" counseling psychologists Faiver et al. (2000) suggest some points of contact. If mental health is a state of balance in the self, then one of those points of balance is between appropriate and inappropriate guilt. The authors define appropriate guilt as "awareness of one's shortcomings that ultimately enhances growth" (p. 157). Inappropriate guilt is "emotional baggage that impedes growth" (p. 157).

The positive functions assigned to recognizing one's guilt include avoiding pride, learning what is ethical, and discovering our limitedness in relation to God. On the negative side, guilt is correlated to the major psychiatric disorders of major depression, PTSD, substance abuse, and OCD.

The authors conclude with a discussion of guilt and healing. Their reflections include the universality of need for forgiveness and reconciliation. The role of the priest in the confessional is one expression of this need, as is the more general role of pastoral care in the church. They also highlight the reconciliation of the community as modeled in Paul's Second Letter to the Corinthians. Also, the secular psychotherapist finds himself in the role of receiving confession. Here is where science and religion meet again. The act of confession is an inherently religious act, yet carried out in the setting with the counselor where "the implications of the client's past and future behavior can be examined in that context" (Faiver et al., 2000, p. 161). The counselor listens to the person's story with ears to hear the themes of brokenness and redemption. In this way, the ways of science and religion are held together (pp. 155-161).

The contributions to the literature on bipolar disorder by pastoral counselors has been limited, but what has been present is the dialogue with the behavioral sciences in understanding and treating mania and depression, and the value of a systems approach to therapy. The best methods seem to be those that include a model of community that is called upon as a resource in giving care, such as the congregation, the mental health services profession, and medical professionals who treat the biological components of bipolar disorder. In this way the systems model involves not only the family but the community at large. Pastoral counseling in this respect is defined as mobilizing all available resources on the client's behalf.

CONCLUSION

> By its very nature [our] work often brings [us] to the threshold of human mystery. It involves sensitivity to the tangled workings of the human mind and heart, and openness to the ultimate concerns that give meaning to people's lives. These areas are of the utmost importance to the church, and call to mind the urgent need for a constructive dialogue between science and religion for the sake of shedding greater light on the mystery of man in his fullness.
>
> Pope John Paul II, 1993

This proclamation by the Holy Father echoed the voice sounded at the Second Vatican Council, "The Church in the Modern World." This council in every way sought to enter the dialogue between religion and science, and offer a way for contemporary Catholics to maintain faith and be enlightened by the onrushing advances in the biological and behavioral sciences. But this was not the first time in the church's history that Scripture and science had open conversation. In his article "The Church and Psychiatry" O'Connell (2001) traces some of the history of this dialogue, beginning with the Rule of Saint Benedict, which taught that those who were ill (including the mentally ill) were to be cared for "above and before every duty." The church in the Middle Ages also cared for the insane in the monasteries. In fact, Saint Thomas Aquinas declared that the treatment of the mentally ill was the province of the church alone, based on the principle that the soul was the locus of the functions of the mind. He was supported in this opinion by the writings of Saint Augustine, most notably in *City of God.*

Throughout most of history the treatment of the insane was cruel and inhumane, and those who needed hospitalization were instead imprisoned. Fortunately, in the Age of Enlightenment there arose a movement for the "moral treatment of the insane." In England and the United States hospitals were founded on these principles by the Quakers, in the nineteenth century. The twentieth century brought what was to be a separation between the treatment of mental illness and the churches, as the science of psychology came to the forefront. First the method of psychoanalysis, then the introduction in the 1950s of the first antipsychotic medications further divided the worlds of science and religion.

The year 1953 saw the first step in gradual reconciliation between the two fields, in an address delivered by Pope Pius XII to the Fifth International Congress on Psychotherapy and Clinical Psychology. In that speech he recognized that "science affirms that recent observations have brought to light hidden layers of the psychic structure of man, and tries to understand the meaning of these discoveries, and to interpret them and render them capable of use" (O'Connell, 2001, p. 17). It was a tremendous move toward understanding and bringing the church into the modern world, but even more importantly it initiated a shift in the way theologians viewed mental illness. They began to move away from a view of insanity as a moral weakness, and toward an understanding of the biological components of mental illness that could be utilized in ministry to sufferers within communities of faith (O'Connell, 2001, pp. 15-17).

Chapter 3

Quaker Treatment of the Mentally Ill

> To provide for the suitable accommodation of persons who are or may be deprived of the use of their reason, and the maintenance of an asylum for their reception, which is intended to furnish, besides requisite medical aid, such tender, sympathetic attention as may soothe their agitated minds, and under the Divine Blessing, facilitate their recovery.
>
> Friends Hospital, Philadelphia
> Mission Statement

The philosophy of the Friends Hospital was and continues to be the "moral treatment" of the psychiatric patient. What that phrase means in the context of the history of mental health care will be explored in this chapter on how Quaker hospitals have treated the mentally ill, often at better rates of success than conventional medical hospitals. It was Quaker theology that informed this method of care and Quaker adherents who spoke out about the injustices of traditional psychiatric care. Moreover, it was Quaker ministers and doctors who heard the call to create something better—a humane treatment for patients who had suffered the indignities of a health care system that neither understood their problems nor sought to do anything but keep them out of sight.

A MODEL

How do pastoral counselors care for the severely disturbed persons in their places of ministry, especially the bipolar client? One might consider the contribution of a Quaker scholar, Zoe White, and her

The Treatment of Bipolar Disorder in Pastoral Counseling

doi:10.1300/5696_04

theology of pastoral care (1998). As cited in the work of Bradstock (2002), White puts forth a model for pastoral care that encompasses the central beliefs of Quakerism. She proposes a pastoral care that (1) is organic (one that is congruous with the self and community), (2) is an ongoing process and not a static offering of help, (3) is a two-way experience between pastor and seeker, (4) recognizes the whole person—body, mind and spirit, and (5) embodies the relationships in the spirit and the presence of healing and wholeness (p. 9).

White provides a blueprint for how the pastoral counselor might help the bipolar client, and understand his or her role in the healing process. The process of healing, as it takes place in the therapist-client relationship, is always in the presence of the light of Christ and the participants enter into periods of silence in which they can apprehend the guidance of Christ. Finally, the healing in the room can only be effective if it includes the community outside the room, and therapists must encourage that connection and not see themselves as the sole agents of healing. Where did White arrive at these concepts? From the founders of the movement that came to be known as the Society of Friends, or Quakers.

THE FOUNDERS

The ideas that formed the nucleus of a dissident Protestant religion began to take shape in the north of England with the teaching of George Fox (1624-1690). Fox's personal experience of faith included a struggle with inner conflict and depression, during which he received healing and a personal conviction that "there is one, even Christ Jesus, who can speak to thy condition" (Weening, 2002, p. 1). What came out of this period was the firm belief that God was in Christ bringing about health and wholeness for those who would believe.

Bradstock (2002) describes Fox's religious conversion as a "new structure" that arose out of his experience of illness and a period of self-examination. Depression was understood as a "temptation" and the recovery from it was accomplished through "honesty, fidelity and earnestness." This was no bootstrap theology, but a developing personal discipline in Fox that gave order to a chaotic mind. His personal experience drove him to teach others about the new light of Christ dwelling in him that brought healing to broken bodies and minds. Fox began to travel and preach about his experience, and the community that grew up around him became known as the Religious Society of Friends (Quakers). The term "friend" came from the idea of friendship with Christ (John 15) and each other.

Edmund Goerke (1964) recounts a number of Fox's healing adventures, and many of them involve the inclusion of the community. In one such event, Fox states:

> And they told me there was some Baptists and a Baptist woman. And John Rush went alongst with me to visit her and when she came there was a many people in the house that was tender about her. And they told me she was not a woman for this world and if I had anything to comfort her concerning the world to come I might. So I was moved of the Lord God to speak to her and the Lord raised her up and she was well to the astonishment of town and country. (p. 1)

This account reveals some of the aspects of Quaker theology that were to find application in the emerging Quaker church, including the importance of a caring community, a community as the locus of healing and health, and the inspiration from God to speak God's word in a particular situation. Fox was to become the founder of a movement that would take as its mission bringing the light of Christ to those in darkness, especially the mentally ill.

Ground was broken in the mission to the mentally ill by the Quaker community at York, England, in 1796. William Tuke had a vision for the care of the insane that included the central notion of the equal value of all persons as created in God's image. He believed that to successfully treat one who is ill of mind, one must hold up a mirror that reflects the image of a worthy person (Whitaker, 2002, p. 24). The experience of mental illness carries with it the impression that a sufferer is less of a person and less valuable in the eyes of others and God. To help a person recover, one must guide the person to a renewed sense of self-worth and a belief in oneself as a child of God. Only then can other treatments have any benefit.

Tuke and his followers established a hospital to which patients could go and live and recover from their illnesses. The philosophy of the hospital was grounded in the religious values of the Quaker community, and sought to "assist nature" in the recovery process, through a daily routine of work, games and social activities, and the arts. In all cases, the goal was to provide as much freedom as possible, humane treatment by the staff, and inclusion in the community life of the hospital, with other patients and staff. The records of the hospital indicate a 70 percent success rate for more acute admissions and a 25 percent success rate (meaning discharge) for more chronic patients. Whether these statistics are reliable is not certain, and whether the rates of success are admirable is debatable. What is astounding is the completely new direction taken in the field of psychiatric care by a group of religious adherents, most not medically trained, who had a word from God about the care of souls and the healing of an injustice.

It was a short time later that the Quakers of Pennsylvania joined the cause to care for the insane in America. Under the leadership of Benjamin Rush and Isaac Bonsall, a hospital was established on a fifty-two-acre farm near Frankford, five miles from the city of Philadelphia.

The new hospital was

> constructed with the York Retreat as its model and William Tuke's principles as its guide. . . . By removing the mentally ill from the outside world . . . these men sought to implant a feeling of stability and a sense of order into the hearts of the insane; thus allowing them a chance to reorder and restructure their lives. (Atta and Roby, 1980, p. 3)

The Frankford Quakers had a clear view of insanity and its treatment. If every person is a child of God, then each has a right to a full relationship with God and the experience of the inner light of Christ. So it is the Quaker mission to remove the roadblock of insanity so that all can have access to the good news of Christ's love. One even gets the sense that this work was felt to be an obligation among Quakers, along with various other reform efforts in society. The Quakers also had a strong bias against the traditional practice of medicine, with its torturous treatment of the insane. The hallmarks of Christian love for patients were compassion and dignity. These high goals were not established in isolation; the presence of the community and the healing power of friends in Christ were recognized as primary. Success rates at this hospital ranged from 50 to 60 percent depending on the severity of the diagnosis and length of illness.

The philosophy of care at this and other Quaker asylums became known as the "moral treatment of mental illness." This meant something very specific to nineteenth-century Quakers, namely, the responsibility of society to care for all of its members as God's own, even those who behaved or appeared strange. The practice of casting them out of society was forbidden by God. The "divine principle" was the backbone of this philosophy, a belief that in all people there was a spark of the Divine Light. It was the duty of those entrusted to care for troubled persons to help them find that light again.

The basic principles of moral treatment were acceptance, occupation, and responsibility. Acceptance meant inclusion as a full member of the community: "The patients were given the opportunity to become stable members of the community . . . patients and staff worked the farm together, ate their meals communally, and resided permanently in the same buildings" (Atta and Roby, 1980, p. 4). Occupation meant the therapeutic value of daily labor: "The men usually working outdoors on the farm and the women sewing or cooking. The success of the entire treatment program was often believed to have been a direct result of the acceptance, by the patient, of this work ethic" (p. 4). Responsibility meant that one was obligated to the community for cooperative behavior. It was hoped that by fostering good social behavior, a newly discharged patient would know how to act in society. In addition, the plan of care in the asylum depended entirely on the successful socialization of patients. One method of practicing being in the community was attending religious services, thus connecting the circle of one's acceptance as a child of God and the cultivation of an experience of God in the community of Quakers (Atta and Roby, 1980, pp. 1-7).

The Friends Hospital in Philadelphia still exists today with much the same philosophy and commitment to care. It has spawned numerous other institutions of mental health care, many in the northeastern United States. One example is the Quakerdale community in New Providence, Indiana, which offers residential and outpatient treatment for adolescents, using a model similar to that of Friends hospitals. They now call their philosophy "holistic." "Programs emphasize physical, intellectual, emotional, social and spiritual well-being. Quakerdale provides an environment where hope and healing through a meaningful relationship with God is shared" (Herman, 2002, p. 1). One may note the continuing influence of the commitment to moral treatment in the reference to physical well-being (occupation) and social and spiritual well-being (responsibility and acceptance).

A THEOLOGY OF QUAKERISM?

Quaker society has no formal theology, and no ascription to creedal formulas or systematic theology. Quakers understand the "limitations of words to express one's deepest experiences" (Weening, 2002, p. 2). A core of common beliefs and practices has shaped Quakers' faith and informed their care of the needy in society, especially the mentally ill.

Robinson (2001) outlines some of the major tenets of Quaker theology. First is the belief in the indwelling spirit of God in every human being, that all individuals have within them the "light of Christ," and that all persons have inherent value and worth that goes beyond our temporal differences. Second are the values of "simplicity, pacifism, and inner revelation." What Quakers believe most strongly is that each person's knowledge of God comes by direct experience; it is not mediated by another. This belief issues in the practice of a simple lifestyle and the commitment to making peace in the world. Third is the mystical component in Quaker worship, understood as the Inner Light and the direct revelation of God to the believer through the mind and the senses. Fourth is concern for the suffering and unfortunate, growing out of the practice of Christian love and goodness. In this context, love means the kind of love shown by Jesus Christ, whom the Quaker seeks to imitate. Fifth is the belief that all aspects of life are sacramental. The sacraments are more than just the practices of worship; they extend to everyday life and the experience of the presence of God in daily activity (p. 3).

One of the most fascinating aspects of Quaker beliefs is the practice of worship. Weening (2002) writes:

> Quaker worship happens when two or more people feel the need to be still together and seek God's presence. . . . In attentive waiting together in silence, Friends can find peace of mind and a renewed sense of purpose for living and joy in wonder at God's creation. (p. 3)

The practice of silence is felt to be necessary in letting go of the pressures of everyday responsibilities, in order to develop inner awareness of the meaning of one's life, to connect with the self and be open to contact with God, and to find relief from anxiety and fear. The unique aspect of this contemplative practice is the group setting. "The listening and waiting in a meeting for worship is a shared experience in which worshipers seek to meet God" (Weening, 2002, p. 3).

George Amoss (1995) sheds light on this way of worship and the aspects of contemplation. He writes of both the inner and outer aspects of meditation in the Quaker tradition: "To be contemplative in the midst of the world is to be one who is detached from delusion and yet passionately attached to the real human beings and the real world which are one's neighbor and one's self" (p. 1). For Amoss the practice of inner awareness must be focused on Christ, who enlightens the soul and shows the true self: "Christ is not present in or with the human being; rather Christ *is* the human being. . . . not for myself alone, but for the world" (p. 3). Amoss is working toward a clear view of the self in solidarity with others, when we die to our false selves and are born again as members of the Body of Christ, able to live with and serve one another. The doctrine of community grows out of the contemplation of the person of Christ and how he dwells in the believer. Having found that true community of those whom Christ has loved, one is impelled to an embrace of others in the world whom Christ has loved, especially the suffering ones.

SILENCE

The practice of silence and the building of community are inseparably linked. What is necessary here is a specific understanding of how Quakers experience silence and what the effect of its regular practice is. Samuel (2001) explains the motivation behind the use of silence in worship. He says that

> silent expectant waiting is not a method, but is an attitude. It is not something we do and control. It is a posture or attitude of openness, when we let God reach us. It is letting go to allow God to shape our relationship with God. It is being in complete receptiveness and anticipation. (p. 1)

The kind of worship the Quakers propose is quite the opposite from most worship in American Protestant churches. Moreover, these concepts stand against the values of our modern society, where a more aggressive approach is encouraged and speaking one's mind is a cherished right. Listening for God to speak to us and waiting until the word comes are unfamiliar for most believers. Silence can even be a frightening experience for someone habituated to a world of noise and chatter. Yet Christ calls us apart from the world and invites us to step aside from the chaos and hear his words of peace.

Damiano (2002) suggests some of the ways that silence may be a benefit to those who commit to its practice. She refers to Thomas Merton's suggestion that it is through our silence that we admit our separation from God and now desire to listen once again to God's communication. She paints a lovely picture of the inner experience of the one in contemplation:

> The more silence becomes part of our lives, the less impulsive we become. We are slowed down. Silence can reconcile the contradictions within us holding them in healthy tension. Often we can internally watch our first response to a situation. The awareness that comes from a grounding in silence allows us to respond more authentically. (p. 2)

There are many other benefits to silent devotion. Damiano calls it "listening to the Inward Teacher." She surmises that God is constantly communicating with us; it is up to us to merely humble ourselves for a minute and listen in. Damiano also discerns a communal component in the benefits of silence. Silence improves the relationships within a group, and prompts each member to share the joys and concerns of all, and to be a more authentic member of the group. The insights that Damiano shares have great relevance to the needs of the bipolar sufferer, especially the benefits of slowing one's pace, reducing impulsivity, and dealing with internal conflict. Also, the difficulty many bipolar patients have in groups often excludes them from receiving the benefits one can gain from a group. The practice of silence in the context of Quaker worship offers them a perfect opportunity for inclusion in a structured format, a practice that will help calm their internal chaos, and a caring community that will value them as a child of God, even through difficult episodes of their illness.

The concept of silence in the Quaker tradition is much deeper than what has been presented so far. Reich (2002) explores the meaning of silence and suggests a four-part model for its varieties:

1. the silence of *reality* in which the believer chooses to be silent before God as a way to be most real, instead of trying to cover up his or her flaws ("inward nakedness");
2. the silence of *reverence* in which one waits respectfully for God's word rather than "rush into His august Presence with our own words";
3. the silence of *recollection* in which one collects the thoughts that have wandered and finds a way back to God through these thoughts; and
4. the silence of *receptivity*, modeled by the disciples in the Upper Room as they waited for the outpouring of the Holy Spirit on the Day of Pentecost (p. 1).

The inspiring aspect of this model is the realistic view of human nature and its needs: our tendency to hide our weaknesses from God, our need to hurry in and go to God with all our concerns at once, our wandering minds that lose us and our connection to God. All of these dynamics portray a real view of persons that the Quaker practices address openly and earnestly.

A final perspective on silence comes again from Amoss (1988) in his thoughts on the "centering" aspect of silence. He writes that ". . . centering happens in us as if by grace. We can only open ourselves to the silence and wait patiently . . . silence is the still, small voice of God. It is the voice of the inward teacher" (p. 5). The central vision here seems to be that of a kind of unity with God that comes through centering. The proof of this unity would be the capacity to love as Christ loved, because the believer and Christ would be one. Here we see striking parallels to the Gospel of John and the unity of Christ with his disciples. As Jesus reveals in John, we did not choose Christ but he chose us (15:16). So if centering happens by grace, then the union of the believer with Christ must also be by grace.

CONNECTIONS AND MODERN EXPRESSIONS

Quaker publications reviewed for this book revealed numerous references to the thoughts of Carl Jung and the similarities in his psychology to Quaker beliefs. Much of this literature explores the connections between Jung's concept of the self and the Quaker concept of the inner light. The *Round Table Review,* a journal of the Friends Conference on Religion and Psychology, published an account of the historical relationship between Quaker scholars and Jungian psychologists (1993). In that review a comparison was drawn that brings to light those aspects of Quaker thought that might be valuable to those who practice psychology or counseling. A Quaker woman, Elined Kotschnig, became intrigued by the ideas of Carl Jung and was part of a group of scholars in Switzerland who studied the mystical elements in Jung's thought. In her comparison of Jungian analysis and Quaker meditation, she wrote that both methods "require an attitude of alert passivity, an opening of the whole being in stillness and waiting, without pre-deciding what is to emerge" (p. 2). Certainly the two streams of thought had their differences, but some central principles were common to both. One such principle was the belief in a continuous revelation of truth through experience, and the necessity to be open to such revelation. This principle expresses the essence of both Quaker worship and psychoanalysis.

In *Jung and the Quaker Way,* Jack Wallis (1992) presented some ways in which the work of Carl Jung actually advanced the thinking of Quaker writers. Jung's work was an impetus for Quakers to move beyond the idea of faith as comfort to faith as transformative for growth and wholeness. The "light within" in Jungian thought was understood as archetypal and thus always present. This idea supported the Quaker concept of the present reality of God at all times. Jung's concept of the collective unconscious is an expression of the believer's desire for union with the creator and all of creation, a concept shared with the goals of contemplation in Quakerism, to be centered in the other (pp. 51-54, 100, 189).

One might find the conversation between psychology and theology uncomfortable, or a bit like comparing apples and oranges. Nevertheless, what Jungian thought was advancing was an affirmation of connectedness, between believers and God, and between all people and all creation. As a tool for reflection on the treatment of the mentally ill, these conversations witness to the necessary joining together of science and religion. Psychology as a science offered rational methods of study directed toward the deepest concerns of people and the quest for meaning in this life. Jung contributed to the cooperation of religion and psychology by establishing common ground and then introducing the insights of analysis in language that engaged religious people and their imaginations.

Quakers throughout the twentieth century had participated enthusiastically in the dialogue with science and learning, and it was in this spirit that a graduate school of clinical psychology grew up at George Fox University in Newberg, Oregon. The publications about this program illustrate how the principles of Quakerism have embraced the principles of psychology and its clinical application. The bulletin encourages interested students to "integrate your faith with a practice in clinical psychology." It lifts up the value of "spiritual and intellectual gifts" and the interactive study of clinical psychology and Christian theology. Of course, the values of the Quaker tradition are front and center. "The university's Quaker heritage places an emphasis on personal integrity, social justice and peacemaking values." By investing its resources in a school to train professional psychologists to treat the mentally ill, the Quaker tradition has come full circle and once again placed itself in the forefront of the treatment of the psychiatric patients of the world. In this setting, the strong tradition that informs the ethos of the school extends to the learning and practice of graduates who will care for the souls of troubled persons.

The dialogue between Quakerism and other religious traditions continues into the new century. George Anderson (2000), a Jesuit scholar, writes about his experience attending a Quaker worship service. Quakerism was not unfamiliar to him, because he attended Haverford College, a Quaker school in Pennsylvania, for his undergraduate work. His study of the founders of the Society of Friends and his observation of the socially active meetings in New York City prompted him to find out more. His experience in worship highlighted the commonalities of Quaker beliefs and his own Jesuit education.

> Finding God's will through prayer and meditation, and bringing it to bear in our daily lives—such a concept is in keeping with Ignatian spirituality, with its emphasis on freeing ourselves from whatever could prevent us from serving God wholeheartedly. (p. 2)

Anderson finds in his contact with the Friends of New York an expression of the deepest beliefs he himself holds. In such occurrences, the making of peace among believers begins.

CONCLUSION

Throughout Quaker history one finds evidence of the two-pronged approach to the treatment of mental illness, an approach reiterated by White (1998) at the beginning of this chapter—the treatment of the whole person, including the spirit, and the importance of a caring community. The remainder of this study will focus on the role of silence and community in the treatment of bipolar disorder. The Quaker approach provides a beginning and an ongoing guide for how pastoral counselors can address the needs of their bipolar clients.

Chapter 4

Silence and Psychotherapy with Bipolar Disorder

JEWELED SILENCE

God embellishes silence and stasis
with jewels of thought
To be worn inside
diadems of devotion
Quiet radiance
In the loud marketplace

Philip C. Kolin (2001)

More than anything else, the manic person craves silence; the silence that quells the noise inside the head and the racing of thoughts that confuse the mind. For the bipolar person, the loud marketplace comes within. The focus of this chapter is an understanding of the nature of silence, psychologically and theologically, and the possible applications of this study to the practice of psychotherapy with persons with bipolar disorder. Psychological resources include the major models of Western psychology and Eastern Buddhist practice. Theological reflection draws upon parallel theories from the Christian, Jewish, and Buddhist traditions that may inform the work of the pastoral counselor. In particular, the literature suggests that these traditions hold a common understanding of the experience of silence and "self-emptying." This is explored in this chapter.

The Treatment of Bipolar Disorder in Pastoral Counseling

doi:10.1300/5696_05

A PERSONAL ANECDOTE

The personal story I told at the beginning of this book has played an important part in shaping my hypothesis that silence in the therapy hour is helpful to the bipolar client. Although bipolar sufferers have many different experiences of their illnesses, and diverse combinations of symptoms, the one overarching commonality is the never-ending mental chaos. It is a chaos that consumes one's mind, distorts one's behavior, and diverts one's attention from normal functioning in the world. It is an experience of perpetual noise and voices and music that will eventually drive one insane. When the noise goes away, it is a precious gift and a release from mental torture.

I described my therapist Michael as using times of silence to stop the flow of words and voices and noise. This practice allowed me to let in those thoughts and ideas that were helpful and healthy. It was a radical departure from previous psychotherapy, which had consisted mostly of talking. It was remarkable that often I experienced days in which that hour of therapy was the only quiet hour of the day. Naturally, that hour bore much fruit in my recovery, offering some peace in a world that demanded talk and noise and voices. This chapter is a search for the meaning of that silent healing and why it worked for me.

ASPECTS OF SILENCE IN RELIGIOUS EXPERIENCE

Most Western Christians are most familiar with a form of worship that includes singing, speaking, doing, eating, drinking, bowing, genuflecting and a myriad of other actions that direct our attention to God and our praise and prayer to Him. What is unfamiliar to most believers in this hemisphere is the cultivation of silence in worshipping God. Americans live in a noisy, busy world, and we worship God in the same manner. However, spiritual writers and directors have brought an opening to quieter ways of addressing God and using silent time as a way to listen to what God says to us. Christians are finding a more contemplative way to practice their faith that is yielding positive spiritual gains.

Certainly, the practice of silence is not new to the Christian Church. The earliest desert fathers and all monastic traditions subsequently practiced forms of prayer and meditation designed to find and maintain intimacy with God. The benefits accrued and the paradoxes understood were written of by theologians such as Teresa of Avila and Meister Eckhart. Maybe most familiar to Christian readers of the mystics is John of the Cross. His expression of the paradox of silence was this: "Silent music, sounding solitude, the supper that recreates and enkindles love." Mystics found that the practice of silence not only enriched their own inner lives but issued in newness of life and more loving relationships.

The Order of Cistercian Nuns of Santa Rita Abbey (2002) have published a description of their way of communal living, and it begins with silence:

> Silence is the womb of that solitude which is the presence of God. The Spirit of the Lord Jesus has endowed us with a charism for silence. . . . silence invites us to communion with one another. Silence is the deep well out of which flows the word. . . . Silence is our gift to one another throughout the years, the breathing of the Spirit, that peace of heart upon which love builds and grows. (p. 1)

The nuns offer a different perspective on the practice of silence, and the benefits available to those who participate. They believe that the mother God gives the gifts of the Spirit and strengthens our bonds with one another. This is no individual pursuit with the goal of personal enlightenment, but rather it is attention to the presence of God that brings peace among friends in Christ.

The nature of this encounter with God in silence can be understood in numerous ways, with Scripture as the guide. Guenther (1995) has written extensively on the experience of silence:

> Yet Scripture tells us that silence is the place of encounter with God. To wait, as Elijah did on Mt. Horeb, requires that we be attentive, that we ignore the noisy distractions and be willing to get through layers of seeming silence until we find real silence. As we wait for God in silence, we begin to notice and celebrate small, subtle things that we commonly dismiss or ignore. . . . In that deep inner silence, we rid ourselves of nonessentials. (p. 603)

In her work as a spiritual director, Guenther has encountered the fears that clients bring when they seek direction and face the need for silence. "True silence is frightening because it leaves us receptive, open and vulnerable. . . . The real culprit is inner noise . . . our prayer of silent attentiveness is assaulted by fleeting, distracting thoughts" (p. 603). This so aptly describes the experience of the troubled person, and in a modest way suggests the inner experience of the manic person. When the client is unable to quiet the mind and feels bombarded by stimuli from the outside, as well as nonstop noise from within, he begins to know the way toward madness. One might imagine how the successful cultivation of an experience of silence in God's presence would bring a return of sanity, and open the way to wholeness.

A treasured figure in the history of Christian spirituality is Thomas Merton. In taking the vows of his Trappist order, he assumed the ways of silence in every aspect of his life. The practice of this discipline and the writing that emerged provide a window into the mind of a mystic and a real sense of what it might be like for any of us to practice silence outside of the monastery. It was Merton's contention that through silence one might discover the true self that is in Christ. Lane (1989) wrote in an article for *Theology Today* that for Merton

> the true self is one that is wholly separate from this fragile image that we try to construct in the imagination of others. It exists in Christ alone. The true self is one that is emptied of the need for authentication; in dying, it lives. Hence, the Zen doctrine of *Sunyata* or emptiness, joined with a Pauline theology of *kenosis,* allowed Merton to abandon the image of the heralded monk. (p. 7)

More will be said later regarding the idea of kenosis, but Lane makes a process observation of Merton in contemplation, that through the practice of silence one discovers the real self and unmasks any false selves.

In Merton's poetry one sees his reverence for silence and what it might mean for the believer's relationship to God. In this poem, Merton likens one's inner silence to the silent expectancy of nature (Lane, 1989, p. 263):

> When no one listens
> To the quiet trees

When no one notices
The sun in the pool.

Where no one feels
The first drop of rain
Or sees the last star

Or hails the first morning
Of a giant world
Where peace begins
And rages end:

One bird sits still
Watching the work of God

One turning leaf,
Two falling blossoms
Ten circles upon the pond.

If one were to sit still and watch the handiwork of God, not just in static observation but with attention to the flowing, ongoing creating of God, then one would find the beauty in silence and the accompanying inner experience of peace. Lane finds a connection for us in the *Tao Te Ching,* to this effect: "The true meaning of life can never be put into words. At its deepest heart, life remains a wordless mystery" (Lane, 1989, p. 264). The person who suffers from mental anguish and a loss of meaning in life can choose a different path toward healing, a path marked not by words but by silence and meditation on the complexity and beauty of life.

The ongoing goal of this book is the exploration of the meaning of silence and its partner the creation of community, in the treatment of persons with manic depression. One who has made a strong connection between these ideas is Parker Palmer, a Quaker theologian and teacher, who reflects on the experience of silence in Quaker worship and what happens to the participant who opens himself or herself to this learning experience. Palmer says:

> I think about two kinds of silence: inner silence and outer silence. There are times you can't dictate the external silence but you can learn to create internal silence if you practice achieving

> it. And you can see and hear a lot of things that you wouldn't if your inner life was filled with static and noise. (Powell, 2001, p. 13)

Regarding the communal dimension of silence he adds: "In silence you have a deeper sense of community or relationship than you sometimes have in the speaking of words" (p. 13). Palmer's reflections here have to do with a discussion on teaching and learning, yet these very same concepts apply to the learning of the ways of the human soul. Too much conversation may obscure what is to be learned on the interior journey. Silent attention to the opportunities for learning must increase one's receptivity to the lessons of life.

Silence can have a healing quality to it, especially in times of crisis. Most of us have been with someone in crisis and not known what to say. It may well be that the hesitancy to speak is an intuitive response to which one should be attentive. Redmont (1995) tells the story of her psychiatric hospitalization with what at first appeared to be panic attacks. She writes of her inability to pray or make use of the words of her religious tradition to find comfort. What brought her some peace was a quiet friend:

> My friend Rosalind was one of the several loved ones who came to visit me in the hospital. When friends came, we talked, often joked, hugged, sometimes walked together. The day Rosalind came, I was weary and not my talkative self. She found me lying on my bed, asked what I wanted, then sat in silence by my side, rubbing my back. Half asleep, I gave thanks for the receiving. (p. 14)

The psychiatric disturbance caused tremendous changes in Redmont's inner and outer life, and her friends coped as best they could. Rosalind somehow knew that talk was going to be no comfort that day, and through silence and touch brought the beginning of healing to a deeply depressed friend. Words could not carry the depth of meaning that the action of healing touch communicated; words, in fact, would have distracted Redmont from receiving her friend's loving care. Silence was the environment in which healing took place. Silence was the best expression of community between the two friends. It also carried the religious expression of the presence of God in the communal reality of friendship.

The avalanche of words in our modern world may do more to divert our attention from God than to bring us to God. In the Buddhist tradition, seekers try to release themselves from the need for words and recognize their limits. Wang (2001) of Rowan University writes about the dialectic of speech and silence in an article for *Philosophy East and West:* "Silence thus marks the boundary of speaking, the limits of language . . . the inadequacy of language runs the risk of never being sufficiently inadequate, otherwise we would all have been satisfied with silence long ago" (p. 83).

The author's study of Chan Buddhism brings out the understanding of silence and speech in this tradition. Wang argues that the two have a nondual relationship, that there is not a clear boundary between speech and silence.

> Chan masters demonstrate that they apply the principle of "interdependent arising" to the issue of speech and silence, presenting a non-isolated, truly relational understanding of speech and silence. Speech and silence thus no longer have their self-identity. One always functions in relation to the other, and each always has its presence in the other. (p. 91)

How might this concept be useful in building a theology of silence for use in the pastoral counseling setting?

First, as the Chan philosophy emphasizes, the single goal of this practice is not the perfection of the technique, but enlightenment. This is wise advice for both counselor and client. If the use of silence is edifying, if it brings one closer to God, then it is a worthwhile pursuit. If silence becomes the focus and not the tool, then changes are necessary.

Second, the idea of the "interplay between speech and silence" is also a good model for the process of therapy. If talk is constant in the fifty-minute session, the client has no chance to reflect on what has been said. The ebb and flow of periods of speech and intervals of silence may be the most effective method for allowing the client to work more deeply into the unconscious process.

Third, the relational understanding of speech and silence is a postmodern conceptualization of what used to be seen as separate functions. This conceptualization is much like the postmodern theological model of the Trinity, in which the persons of the Trinity are not separate entities but are interdependent and have internal conversation with one another. This parallel suggests a fresh way for the pastoral counselor to interpret to the client a deeper, transcendent perspective on the therapy process. If God is a relational being and the ways of the universe are relational as well, then the path to healing and wholeness must be relational also, in accordance with the interdependence of all things.

PRAYER AND SILENCE

The practice of silent prayer is not something alien to Western Christians. Most believers have, at one point in their corporate worship, time for silent confession or silent intercession for others. A form of silent prayer that has long been practiced in the monastic tradition is the centering prayer. Sandman (2000) describes this approach to God:

> Centering prayer is a remarkably simple method that opens one to God's gift of contemplative prayer. Its practice expands one's receptivity to the presence and activity of God in one's life. . . . The practitioner has the intention to rest deeply in God in silence and to let go of the thoughts, emotions, memories, images or sensations that will inevitably come into awareness during prayer. (p. 12)

Certainly this is a mode of prayer that recognizes the relationship of silence and words. It seeks to deal with the intrusion of words on a time of rest and communion with God. Sandman suggests some of the benefits for one who will take on this practice of prayer:

> God acts within us to transform us, making us more like Christ . . . some may first notice that their life has begun to reflect the gifts of the Holy Spirit . . . to become more deeply centered in our true self where God resides . . . we take a vacation from the false self . . . we make it easier for God to heal the false self in us . . . an ability to love others more selflessly. (p. 14)

The finding of the self in therapy is a thread that runs through most models of psychotherapy. Here is a powerful vehicle for a client involved in such a search. One might expect the unveiling of a false self in centering prayer to be a powerful emotional experience. A wise pastoral counselor will be prepared to create a safe holding environment for such a revelation.

It has been amazing to witness the vitality in descriptions of centering prayer across religious boundaries. In some Jewish traditions, the presence of words in the rigidly prescribed prayer service might seem devoid of any centered awareness of God within. Alan Lew (2000) dispels that notion and opens our eyes to the beauty of prayer in his tradition. He observes,

> . . . I think the real spirituality of the service lies elsewhere—in the rhythm of the service, in the flow of gesture and sound, and in the silence between and behind the language. Spirituality is non-verbal and a-rational. Understanding can certainly enhance it, but can never contain it, nor even convey it very well. (p. 93)

Later in this article he gives a breathtaking interpretation of the actions of the service:

> The stepping back and forward [before reciting the Amidah] is a physical reinforcement of the belief that one is entering another space, a sacred space in which one can encounter God. This is not just an idea; it has a physical reality; it is something we do with our bodies. . . . When we pray, we stand at the nexus between self and other. (p. 95)

Lew describes prayer as "mindfulness activity"; that is what he is describing here. The actions of the body, especially those belonging to a tradition thousands of years old, bring the mind to receptiveness and a mindfulness of God in the midst.

The word "mindfulness" appears frequently in the literature of meditation. It may describe the process of healing for the bipolar client better than any other. Psychologist Steve Shealy (2002a) offers a metaphor for the manic mind and an application of the practice of mindfulness. He writes:

> the mind is a wild horse which has been encouraged to run freely. It loves to run fast, wildly chasing after first this thought, then that sensation, then on to the next bit of stimulation and on into the sunset it runs. Our focused observation brings it from the dark forests and grassy plains into a small pasture with no place to hide. (p. 1)

The therapeutic value of the silence and attentiveness is this:

> we can systematically tame the mind and as we do, free ourselves from its chaotic, distractive tendencies. We can move into a seat of quiet observation in the center of the storm of the mind. We can then capture more moments as they unfold, spend less time in the illusion of past and future, become less reactive and more responsive in everything we do. (p. 1)

Equally as important for the bipolar sufferer is controlling behavior and its negative consequences. Shealy suggests that through mindfulness one sees that "wise actions lead to greater clarity, peace and freedom, unwise actions lead to less" (p. 1).

So much in this description of centering prayer is pertinent to this discussion. The inner experience of chaos is exactly like that wild horse, the wild chasing-after of thoughts and feelings, the pursuit of temporary pleasure. To picture oneself sitting in a quiet seat in the middle of the mental chaos seems an unreal possibility for the manic person. Nevertheless, Shealy is showing the way to that position via prayer that makes one the observer and not the reactor. In mania, the moments of the day fly by and one is left feeling missed. The mindfulness prayer leads one to a place where one can be with the moment. Finally, focusing the mind on the realities of human behavior allows intentional choices to be made where once the impulses ruled. Seeing consequences clearly in the mind offers the client self-control and self-respect. Shealy uses the theological concepts of peace and freedom quite appropriately in speaking of a state of shalom, of wholeness and health and oneness with God. Once again, as pastoral counselors, we can bring depth to the work on psychological issues through this practice, and the new experience of peace and freedom that it potentially holds.

Centering prayer is practiced in many religious contexts, yet in each there is emphasized the regular discipline of daily prayer and the benefits that come when such a discipline is maintained. Jonas (2002) tells the story of his meeting with the Dalai Lama and their discussion of the practice of prayer. In reference to his daily routine, Jonas write that,

> each morning he arises before dawn to meditate and to pray, and he finds additional quiet times each day. But in a way, he is always meditating, very much in the flow of what we Christians would call "unceasing prayer." (p. 4)

Another aspect of the master's way of prayer is the focus on compassion, one part of which is a call to community: the second part of the way of compassion is "opening to genuine empathy and connectedness to others, even our enemies" (p. 5). It is a wonderful dialectic of detachment and connection that typifies the nature of Buddhist meditation, and an ever-present use of paradox to bring enlightenment to the life of the believer. The theme of freedom also arises here, with the pursuit of freeing one's self from attachment to material items and being free for connection to others. For the psychiatric patient, finding freedom from the struggles of life in the material world and freedom for intimacy with persons who will accept and love without condition is a lifesaving discovery.

The past thirty years in this country have seen a flowering of study and dialogue regarding the role of faith in healing. In 1975 Dr. Herbert Benson of the Harvard Medical School published a book, *The Relaxation Response,* that told the story of his own work with patients on the use of meditation in their treatment for cardiovascular problems. In his research, he was curious about students he knew who practiced Transcendental Meditation and wondered what the effects on their heart rates and respiration would be. What he found was revolutionary for the study of mind-body connections. The scientific journal *Technology Review* interviewed Dr. Benson in 1996 and asked him about the results of his work.

In reflecting on the meaning of his findings, he said:

> we studied more people, asking them simply to repeat the number "one," or to say a prayer, and found the same physiological changes. This boils down to a mind-body link with therapeutic implications: if you think in a certain way, then measurable, predictable, and reproducible physiological changes will occur that are opposite to the fight-or-flight response. (p. 35)

Benson stresses that the self-care component can enhance the effect of other modes of treatment. As a medical doctor he is concerned with the health and well-being of the whole person. Yet his approach opens the door more widely to the belief that religion can contribute to the health and healing of patients who have a practice of faith. "My idea is to use the relaxation response to counteract the harmful effects of stress and couple it with the power of belief, which I also call remembered wellness, to enhance its efficacy" (Benson, 1996, p. 39).

The possibility that prayer might have a healing effect on physical illness gives great hope to believers of all faiths whose hope wanes in the face of physical or mental deterioration. Benson lends scientific credibility to the conviction that people of faith have always held, namely, that one's relationship to God is central to one's health and wholeness.

However, not everyone engaged in the dialogue between science and religion has a need. The questions raised about the connections between science and faith come from both sides of the debate. At a 1996 Conference on Spirituality and Healing in Medicine at Harvard Medical School, researchers presented papers documenting the rift between religion and medicine. David Larson of the National Institute for Healthcare Research told the conference that fewer than 1 percent of research in medicine "includes the most basically acceptable type of spiritual or religious commitment variables in published studies" (Culligan, 1996, p. 18). Moreover, concern was expressed about how open dialogue might affect each of the participants. Culligan (1996) reported in the journal *America*:

> Are prayer and meditation to be understood only in a utilitarian frame—simply as ways to reduce tension? Many at the Boston conference feared that the dialogue between religion and medicine would, in the end, trivialize religion by misleading people into thinking that its sole purpose is to promote good physical and mental health. (p. 17)

Culligan encouraged religious communities to foster what Gordon Allport called "intrinsic religion," a practice of faith that nurtures the inner life as the way toward wholeness. The warning here is that a utilitarian practice of meditation is merely an outward sign of religiosity and an inauthentic expression of faith. Only the inward way to God can bring true wholeness.

SELF-EMPTYING AS A WAY TOWARD HEALTH

In Christian spirituality is a tradition of prayer that will change the life of the person who through it seeks change. One such stream of teaching focuses on the biblical notion of "kenosis" or "self-emptying." The origin of this concept is in the Letter of Paul to the Philippians, Chapter 2, where Paul cites a Christian hymn that celebrates Christ's emptying of himself and taking the form of a servant. Naturally, "kenosis" is a word that invites multiple interpretations, and that is its beauty. Christians over the centuries have plumbed the depths of this word and have incorporated it into the mystical tradition of the Church. Eastern religions have also used this idea, because it resonates with their understanding of emptiness as a way to enlightenment.

What meanings have been attached to this brief hymn, what might it mean for modern believers, and what is it about this image that might contribute to the practice of silence, centering prayer, and meditation as ways toward wholeness for the mentally ill? One may begin with how it was used in the ancient church. Lounibos (2000) reviews the concept of kenosis in an article for the *Journal of Pastoral Counseling*. He begins with the writing of Thomas Merton and his understanding of the path to the true self through the self-emptying of Christ. Lounibos's study of the multiplicity of meanings in kenosis is especially useful. He examines the Gospels for ways in which the Gospel writers incorporate this theology to tell their story, including the Passion narratives, the Last Supper, the Washing of Feet, and the "first must be last" sayings. Lounibos writes:

> the kenosis of Christ was his life of service for the poor, the sick, the stranger, the other, the little ones. John places the crucifixion on the day before the Passover to symbolize the comparison between the death of Jesus and the slaughter of the Paschal lambs, a kenosis that liberates, rescues, and saves the first and second Israel. (p. 3)

Lounibos builds his Christology, incorporating a psychological understanding by exploring the meaning of *self*. What is unique about the person of Jesus is his willingness to empty himself and take on servanthood. One must wonder what it was about Jesus that allowed him to integrate such a radical self-image. Lounibos suggests that is was a focus on truth:

> It is our human task to continually empty ourselves of falsely formed images and concepts of our relation to God and others and restore the proper rhythms of self-emptying that allows for

> God's gracious filling. God's favor, blessing or grace is both emptying and filling. Emptying and filling are two aspects of the same divine self-communication. (p. 4)

Lounibos has some extraordinary insights into the nature of self. The most powerful is the paradoxical benefit of self-emptying. For what is emptied are unhealthy constructs of the self, and what is taken in is a healthier, relational self that is integrated with God's grace. Once again the two sides of the spiritual life, being filled and giving to others, find their expression in a simple hymn about a simple act in Jesus' life. The ego is a social and spiritual reality.

Brown (1999) finds the concept of kenosis a profitable way to rethink the nature of God.

> The homoousia of the Son with the Father indicates not merely a static unity of substance, as traditionally understood, but rather a single, dynamic, kenotic nature in which Father and Son share one function or non-dual function of self-emptying . . . in God's identification with all things, there is no self-withholding on God's part. God gives himself completely and is absolutely accessible. Indeed, God is most truly God in this self-emptying. (p. 12)

If the truth about God is that his entire nature is self-giving, this truth creates a whole new picture in the mind of the believer who once thought of God as a distant and unemotional being. The kenotic God's very nature is to give of himself. There is no other way that this God can be toward his creatures.

Much has been said in contemporary theology regarding the internal relations of the Trinity, and this is stated most clearly in the work of Jürgen Moltmann. What is applicable here is the inclusion of kenosis. Brown (1999) interprets it this way:

> God is not subject, but community, the inner life of which is kenosis . . . this divine kenosis is being as well as non-being. It is neither being nor non-being. It is the unfathomable secret of love, which one cannot comprehend, but rather only worship in amazement. Because all our notions create idols, only amazement understands the secret of reality. (p. 13)

The meaning of a God who empties himself for us can only be apprehended in a life that cultivates silence. This idea of God is too great to be understood through study; it only means something in the context of a life that has brokenness in it. The broken spirit needs a God who will come down and walk with the person through the dark valley. The kenotic God does this not from time to time, but continually, as the expression of this. What God did in Christ Jesus was empty himself of power to serve a people whom He loved. Just as the people of Israel heard from Moses about their election (Deuteronomy 7:7-11), so all believers face the reality of a God who acts not by throwing thunderbolts but by coming down and living like us that we might be one with Him. For people who suffer with a psychiatric disorder, it may be incomprehensible that God would choose to love them in spite of what they have done or thought. It may be even more astounding to realize that God cares for them out of His own nature and nothing is forced. Here is where pastoral counseling has a purpose: to help sufferers to calm the inner chaos through the practice of silence, and then guide them to a new experience of God who is for them and not against them. In the context of such an experience, healing is possible.

The Dalai Lama's call to compassion belongs in this context also. Compassion, according to the Master, is a way of prayer, and a way of community. On the internal side of the experience of compassion is what Friedland (1999) calls "a mental state in which one takes the suffering of another as her or his own. . . . One person is able to gain a deeper insight into the inner life of another" (p. 35). Compassion is a way for the pastoral counselor to practice psychotherapy. Entering into a mental state that allows one to feel what another feels takes great preparation and prayer, but the benefits to the client will be many times greater. Friedland calls this process "equanimity," which he describes in this way:

> . . . the achievement of a compassionate way of life requires developing a balanced state of mind in which one is focused without being fixated on any particular impermanent phenomenon. . . . Equanimous awareness is open to acknowledge events as they occur instead of being biased by some intimate set of distractions. (p. 35)

Truly this approach has far-reaching implications for therapists, as it addresses many of the problems they experience. The inner turmoil of distractions, fixations, and imbalances constantly looms over the process of therapy, threatening to subvert the process. Compassionate mindfulness and the emptying of self will calm the mind of the therapist so that she may connect with the inner turmoil of the client. Moreover, the practice of compassion applies not only in the counseling room but in the therapist's entire life. Compassion becomes more than a technique; it becomes a healing way of being in which the client is invited to participate. This method of therapy might be called an anti-method, that is, a noncontrolling approach that gives clients back the control they have lost. It is a way to freedom that involves the work both of client and therapist; for to live out the demands of compassion will take much work on the therapist's part. Friedland reflects on the idea of freedom through compassion:

> Equanimity allows one to feel compassion for the suffering of others without becoming overwhelmed or by neglecting it. It constitutes a precise awareness of present situations in which there is no grasping. Being thus free of mental attachments, it is possible to have a much greater sensitivity to all the interpersonal events of inner life. (p. 35)

SILENCE AND PSYCHOTHERAPY

The use of silence in psychotherapy is not a strange idea. Silence has always been a part of psychoanalysis and other psychodynamic therapies that focus on the unconscious and its access through free association. It has been a standard tool for pastoral counselors and spiritual directors in their work with clients in spiritual crisis who want to reconnect with God. In the Eastern traditions, silence allows access to the self and the reality of the emptiness of the self. In all of these settings, the client is generally neurotic or fairly healthy, and not suffering psychosis. Is the use of silence appropriate for the psychotic client, or for one who has a major psychiatric disorder like manic depression?

Bogart (1991) published a review of the literature on meditation and psychotherapy and his results will guide this exploration of the application of silence to the care of the mentally disturbed. First is the question of the use of meditation in therapy. Bogart found that it helped the client to "know their own processes" to "bring a state of relaxation . . . an altered state of consciousness" (p. 2).

Silence helps in the cultivation of awareness and memory, of feelings and images that come directly to the mind, and not through talk. Meditation provides "abundant material for the exploration of therapy" and "working with inner turmoil" (p. 3). Long-term benefits exist as well: telling the truth, releasing negative emotions, authenticity, trust, integrity, wholeness, and the capacity to give and receive love. Certain cognitive benefits were also mentioned, such as the "deautomatization of consciousness," "cutting away false cognitive certainties" and "perceptual expansion" (p. 6).

One criticism of the blending of psychology and spirituality in therapy is that it will relieve the client of responsibility for tackling the difficult issues of their emotional history. A helpful distinction was the model of psychotherapy as work toward integration of the self, while meditation is work toward the transcendence of the self. Another view suggests that psychotherapy and meditation are "not related in a linear sense . . . but act synergistically to promote human growth" (Bogart, 1991). Jung wrote about the problems that ensue when a person is "overwhelmed by the unconscious through improper use of Eastern psychotechnologies" (quoted in Bogart, 1991, p. 12). His concern was the possible exacerbation of psychotic symptoms and the flood of unconscious images that the mind cannot process without expert help.

Having looked briefly at the Western ways of integration of meditation, we turn now to the riches in the Buddhist tradition of inner exploration and the ongoing dialogue between Buddhism and depth psychology. In an article on integration of meditation and psychotherapy, Burns (2002) explains the centrality of the mind in Buddhism: "If the basis of Christianity is God, the basis of Buddhism is the mind. From the Buddhist viewpoint, mind or consciousness is the core of our existence" (p. 1). Burns also recognizes the interdependence of mind and body in Buddhism, and that the problems of existence must be the concern of religion. One such problem is suffering, and one aspect of meditation in the Buddhist tradition is the relief from suffering and its effect on human consciousness.

The question remains of the value of meditation to the psychological health of human beings. The answer given by Burns is that the practice of meditation contributes to human growth and maturity. The two goals of Buddhist meditation, goals that are shared with the practice of depth psychology, are

> first, the increase, enhancement and cultivation of positive feelings such as love, compassion, equanimity, mental purity and the happiness found in bringing happiness to others. Secondly . . . the relinquishment and renunciation of greed, hatred, delusions, conceit, agitation, and other negative, unwholesome states. (p. 3)

In addition, cognitive goals are to be pursued, including nonattachment, insight, and concentration. Each of these aims weds the spiritual experience of the unconscious with the healthy function of the mind. Since in Buddhism the working of the mind is the focus of meditation, then the practice of meditation according to Buddhist principles might be supportive of the work of any form of psychotherapy with the same goals—nonattachment, insight, and concentration.

Meditation takes full account of the feelings of the subject, and teaches him or her to be present to his or her feelings and not overanalyze them. Psychiatrist Mark Epstein (1998) writes about the use of feelings in meditation and the parallels to psychotherapeutic practice. He recognizes the place of feelings in Western therapy and what they mean: "If we want to live a full life . . . we must recover the capacity to feel . . . by surrendering to who we really are . . . we are afraid of falling apart . . . we have not learned how to give up control of ourselves" (p. 46). Using the image of the "holding environment" (D. W. Winnicott), the author describes the place of meditation as a safe place in which the mind could be free to simply observe one's feelings. The term "mindfulness" is used to show the nature of awareness that must exist in the person. The goal is then to allow difficult feelings to come into awareness and learn to tolerate them. By doing this, the client integrates these feelings into his or her self and can heal from their negative effects.

Epstein also explores emptiness as a true, human experience. Again, allowing the feelings of emptiness into consciousness will make its integration possible. If the client can accept feelings instead of analyzing or moralizing, then healing happens in the deeper parts of the soul. Epstein writes about the "internal chatter" that one confronts when beginning meditation and how it is gradually let go. He is not referring to the bipolar experience of racing thoughts and internal voices, but his insights are highly relevant to this experience. Nothing can give a person deep in mania more relief than learning to sit quietly and still the chatter that drives him or her to madness (pp. 46-50).

Steve Shealy (2002b) characterizes the relationship between psychotherapy and meditation as a "dance" and a "synergistic and dynamic" process (pp. 1-2). Having studied the two fields in relationship, one can draw some conclusions about the value of meditation for pastoral counseling, and for treating bipolar clients.

First, clients who come for pastoral counseling, and even those who seek out their minister for pastoral care, are in many ways confronting the presence of emptiness in their lives. It disturbs them and drives them to behaviors that are unhealthy—addiction, depression, affairs, overworking and overfunctioning, and many others. The traditional methods of talk therapy may help the client perceive this truth, but meditation may help them truly experience it and begin to change. This practice allows the full depth of the experience of existential emptiness by being present to it. One can integrate it into the healthy personality.

Second, meditation can facilitate self-awareness in ways that psychotherapy can only address superficially. A client can know intellectually about his or her fears and doubts, but cannot be fully aware of them without being in a state of mindfulness that allows the mind to quiet the other competing voices and hear only the truth. If part of pastoral counseling is truth-telling, then meditation can assist in telling a truthful story.

Third, the reality of suffering in the world and within the self is something most clients would wish to avoid. Yet it is the most profound of spiritual problems and one that will be ultimately confronted in one's life. Psychotherapy can address the problem of suffering and provoke the initial feelings, but meditation may truly allow the client to plumb the depths of universal suffering. It can be tempting for the client in pain to split off the reality of suffering from his or her "normal" life; psychotherapy's goal would be to help the client reintegrate the two. Meditation can be the tool that starts the process.

Fourth, for the bipolar client, all these situations apply to their experience, with one added consideration. The internal experience of the manic person is extremely chaotic. The racing thoughts and psychotic symptoms bring inner havoc, and the mania induces impulsive behaviors that may endanger the person's life. In traditional psychotherapy, the goal would be to gain some insight into the source of the problem, to modify the more extreme behavior, and find an appropriate medication to stabilize moods and psychotic symptoms. In this context, meditation can be a supportive therapy in calming the mind of the client. Once a state of mindfulness is achieved, then the awareness of feelings, including anger and rage against suffering, is allowed to emerge, and the therapist can help the client to accept the feelings and integrate the experience of mental anguish into the picture of who he or she is, his or herself.

Finally, the practice of silence with the bipolar client may allow him or her for the first time to slow down enough to have a real experience of God. In this chapter, the images of communion with God in silence and the beauty and peace one finds in silence are highlighted as benefits. If the manic-depressive person has never been quiet enough to hear the voice of the Spirit speaking in their heart, then to find it in the pastoral counseling setting can be transforming. The pastoral counselor has a unique opportunity to help a client find relief from the mania that obscures the beauty in life, that "peace of God which passes all understanding" (Phillippians 4:7 NRSV).

Chapter 5

Community in Treatment

Another point of intersection between psychology and pastoral counseling in the care of the mentally ill is the role of the patient's community. By community we mean all the ways in which a person is in relationships—family, marriage, church, friendships, and the larger society. Psychology has embraced the value of community in the family therapy movement, the support group explosion, and the twelve-step method of treatment with alcoholics. Pastoral counseling finds its inclusion of community informed by the biblical notions of the people of Israel in Exodus and the community of the early church in Acts. In both disciplines, the individual finds healing and wholeness in the context of a community that nurtures them and instructs them. The aim of this chapter is to illustrate these ideas more fully and consider them as a way of healing for the client with bipolar disorder.

CASE STUDY

Terry was a forty-year-old white male who came to the family therapy clinic with problems with impulsive behavior. He said that he had been stealing items from convenience stores, gambling on sports, and having sex almost daily with prostitutes. He seemed like a calm, softspoken man and it surprised me that he would act in these ways. When I began to ask our assessment questions, he revealed that he suffered from manic-depressive illness and was on two medications, lithium and desipramine. He also said he had been recovering from alcoholism for the past fifteen years, and that his Alcoholics Anonymous (AA) group had been his major source of support throughout that time.

Terry was married and had four children, with a fifth on the way. He also had an adult son from a previous relationship who lived with the family. Terry Jr. and his dad were close, but Dad saw the same characteristics in his son

The Treatment of Bipolar Disorder in Pastoral Counseling

doi:10.1300/5696_06

that he saw in himself and it scared him. Terry seemed quite devoted to his wife and children, in spite of his reckless behavior, and spent a great deal of time with his kids, all boys. It was difficult to make sense out of this scenario, until I began taking some family history.

Terry was raised in a family with two parents and one brother. His memories of childhood were traumatic, and included being kidnapped at age five. He recalled feeling afraid all the time and ignored by his parents. When he became older, he began to notice his parents' constant parties and their exchanging of sex partners. When Terry was about eleven or twelve, his father forced him to participate in these "parties." He was sexually abused on a regular basis—by women and men—until he was fourteen, when he left home and never returned. During the rest of his teen years he was cared for by an uncle and aunt who provided a stable, safe home and a haven from the abuse of his parents.

In therapy, Terry came to see how much these childhood traumas had affected his emotional development and were the seeds for his adult behavior. As we worked together it seemed that he was letting go of the gambling and stealing, but still struggled with his sexual behavior. One Tuesday afternoon he failed to show for an appointment. This was unusual for him. When I called and spoke to his wife, she informed me that Terry was in jail on charges of child molestation. She believed they would be able to get bail together and get him released in a few days.

He came to his therapy appointment the next week and told me the story of the arrest and denied all of the charges. As we continued to meet over the next few weeks the trial process went on and he continued to claim that he had been falsely accused by their neighbor, with whom he had had much conflict. In what turned out to be our last session together, Terry related the likelihood that he would be convicted and sent to state prison, most likely for fifteen to twenty years. He was terrified of this possibility, as he had heard how sex offenders were treated in prison. He feared leaving his wife and family behind with no means of support. We had so much to work on, but no time to resolve anything.

For Terry, the issue of community was key to coping with bipolar disorder. He had three significant communities—his wife and family, his pastor and church, and his AA meetings. His family was a source of unconditional love and a purpose for living. Terry's love for his wife and children was strong and deep. Without this connection he would have had no reason to live. Terry was active in his church and had a good relationship with his pastor, someone he could go to during the times when he wanted to drink. His AA group was a close-knit community of people who had been in recovery for many years. They were often a lifeline for Terry when he was in trouble.

What was difficult to explain was why, with so much support, Terry so often made mistakes. The answer may lie in the nature of mania and impulsive behavior. If he went off his medications, the impulsive behavior was automatic. No rational explanation existed for the reckless acts committed in these states. Nevertheless, it was the community that brought Terry back down from binges and back to sanity.

COMMUNITY IN THE SOCIAL SCIENCES

The mystery of mental illness includes understanding how it is that a person gets better. In this book, we have had extensive discussion of the biological and psychotherapeutic methods of treatment, and a proposal regarding how prayer and meditation might be a supportive therapy. What is becoming clearer in the social sciences, especially social psychology, is the contribution of the patient's community to their recovery. The individual models of the previous generation have opened the doors to include psychosocial models of etiology and treatment.

Psychologist Ronald Bassman (2001) describes his own journey of recovery from schizophrenia and the treatments he received that were most effective and humane. He sees himself as a "psychiatric survivor" and in a continual "process of transformation" (p. 34). He asks the question, "Do we recover or are we transformed by our experiences?" (p. 34). He leaves that distinction to the opinion of the person in recovery. Most important to him are those things that made a difference in his treatment. His experience parallels that of other patients he interviewed, who said that what helped them was "a person who told them that they have a chance to get better. Having someone believe in them translated into hope. . . . Hope fights fear and nurtures courage. It inspires vision and the work required to realize the unattainable" (p. 38). In this process healing takes place in caregivers as well; for they will be changed and healed of their own prejudices when they work with a mentally ill person. "By demystifying madness, we can begin to appreciate the beautiful gifts that diversity offers to everyone" (p. 40).

Bassman takes the risk of revealing his illness in the hope that his story will reach other patients and families who seek the best treatment. What he does most of all is establish community with the readers by self-revelation and honest appraisal of the outcomes. He seeks to do what others have done for him—to tell other sufferers that they have a chance to get better. If hopelessness is the roadblock to recovery, then the best antidote is the story of one who has journeyed from illness to health. If he can do it, so can another patient. It is fascinating that he identified not psychotherapy or medication first, but relationships with others as the primary need for patients. He does not devalue the scientific therapies, but simply raises the power of the community to the same level. Healing requires both.

A factor to consider in the process of recovery is how we define quality of life. Certainly the pursuit of a full and rewarding life is a reason for entering psychotherapy. For the person with severe psychiatric disturbance, the meaning of quality and the expectation of reasonable outcomes may be different, and difficult to assess. Angermeyer et al. (2001) studied this issue in their article for the *International Journal of Social Psychiatry*. Their task was to compare how psychiatrists defined quality of life for their patients, how patients defined it for themselves, and what the differences might mean.

On the one hand, the doctors' chief concerns were reducing the effects of neuroleptic medications (which can be severe), social integration and participation, social contacts and relationships, social acceptance and competence, and the involvement of the patient's family. On the other hand, the patients defined quality of life as having meaningful work, good health, leisure pursuits and social contacts, independence, a significant committed relationship, and emotional balance (pp. 34-42). When a comparison was made of the two samples, it was noted that the two categories most highly correlated were the areas of work and social contacts. The doctors focused more on the medical aspects of a whole life and patients seemed to be more concerned with the daily functions of living an independent life. It is noteworthy that both samples held high the value of community in defining a high-quality life. This definition is narrow enough that one may use the criteria for quality as an ongoing reminder as this paper proceeds. The proposal of ideas regarding treatment for mental illness is an empty task without the awareness of the hopes and dreams of the patient.

Since the deinstitutionalization of psychiatric patients began in the 1960s, mental health professionals have been concerned with the adequacy of care in community settings. One such concern was for patients who were called "day care" psychiatric patients. In a recent study of these patients in Hong Kong, Tam et al. (2000) observed the aspects of care that were most beneficial to the patient's self-concept. The authors write that "the rediscovery and reconstruction of an enduring sense of self as an active and responsible agent are important aspects of improvement" (p. 202). However, challenges to the development of positive self-image in the community exist: "Mental illness acts as a negative stimulus and leads to social discrimination" (p. 203). In spite of these problems, the availability of social interaction for the patient still has great advantages. Without this resource, self-concepts and levels of personal growth were lower. In an interesting comparison, it was found that in some cases the patients who were still hospitalized had better social interaction than the day care patients. This finding shows the need for better attention to the social needs of patients living in the community (pp. 202-209).

Social psychologists Bengtsson-Tops and Hansson (2001) studied the social networks of schizophrenic patients living in the community, and found them lacking. The authors evaluated patients' social networks using the criteria of "content, intensity and reciprocity." Social networks were understood to include relationships outside the family that support the family in caring for the patient and providing the patient with significant social interaction. They observed few contacts with friends, and it appeared that family members provided most of the social support. Even more significant was the connection between symptoms and community: "More severe negative and positive symptoms were related to a worse social network" (p. 67).

A constant concern for mental health professionals is obtaining compliance with treatment from the patient. Some evidence demonstrates that the presence of a supportive community will increase compliance. Agarwal et al. (1998) studied the contributing factors in compliance and found that "the presence of a key person in the community is crucial to improve compliance" (p. 92). For the severely disturbed, compliance with medication is absolutely necessary for improvement and preventing relapse.

The help of a professional person or friend can improve compliance. When compliant patients were studied, Agarwal and colleagues observed "more supervision and support from a key relative who was available when needed" (p. 96). An important part of the social network can be the social worker, who supervises community care and reinforces the necessity of taking medications. For persons taking neuroleptic medications, the side effects of which are troubling, it is difficult to maintain compliance, without which relapse is certain (pp. 92-106).

Persons with schizophrenia or bipolar disorder may experience repeated hospitalizations for their conditions, and may become frustrated by their inability to get better. A team of rehabilitation psychologists studied this phenomenon and concluded that the most important factor in preventing readmission was the environment the patient returned to after discharge from the hospital. Yamada et al. (2000) concluded that "the environment must be altered in order to accommodate a person's disability and support optimal functioning" (p. 32). They cite a number of components of a good social situation, including a "structured living arrangement," and "freedom, autonomy, stability, security and privacy." Also, the patient who "lives in a parent's house or relative's home, group home or supported housing type of residence may have greater levels of support in closer proximity, than individuals who live independently" (p. 37).

What is critical to the improvement of the patient and prevention of relapse is an environment that helps the patient build a functional life and a connection to others who care unconditionally. Community in this sense has a specific meaning—a caring group of friends and family who cooperate in helping all members find fullness of life, as each understands it.

PUBLIC PERCEPTION OF MENTAL ILLNESS

Probably the biggest obstacle to the formation of community around the psychiatric patient is exaggerated public perception of the behavior of these patients. Automatic reactions include social distancing ("not in my backyard") and stereotyping of the patient as dangerous to society. Link et al. (1999) surveyed the general public regarding their ideas about mental illness and found attitudes that may prevent the mentally ill from finding adequate treatment and support. They summarize public attitudes as follows:

> Mental illness is a very threatening, fearful thing and not an idea to be entertained lightly about anyone. Emotionally, it represents to people a loss of what they consider to be the distinctively human qualities of rationality and free will, and there is a kind of horror in dehumanization. As both our data and other studies make clear, mental illness is something that people want to keep as far from themselves as possible. (p. 1328)

The public perception seems to include a fear that the mentally ill will become violent. People are unwilling to interact socially with someone whose behavior is peculiar, for fear that that person will turn violent. Whether or not this perception is valid, it remains operative in society and a detriment to building community. Without supportive community, the patient has little chance of attaining quality of life and preventing relapse.

There is even a misconception, or overgeneralization, about the competence of psychiatric patients to function independently in society. The laws of this country concerning mental incompetence reveal the underlying attitudes toward the mentally ill and the entrenched fear of their inclusion in society. Pescosolido et al. (1999) designed a survey of public opinion that revealed three assumptions inherent in American society: (1) people with mental disorders are not competent to make autonomous decisions; (2) mental disorders may place a person at increased risk of physically harming himself or herself or others; and (3) coercion inherent in state intervention to redress incompetence or to reduce risk is justified (pp. 1339-1345).

As one analyzes these assumptions, one can see how unspoken human beliefs become encoded in public law and serve to inhibit the building of a tolerant society that includes marginalized members, such as the mentally ill. Popular culture may contribute to the generalizations made by citizens about psychiatric illness. Yet that same culture reflects the unconscious fear of the general populace, the fear that this potential may lurk within them or their families.

The opportunities for establishing community on behalf of the mentally ill are many, yet the obstacles are large. The social sciences have illumined the present situation and recommended changes for the future. The following sections explore religious and spiritual motivations for these changes and the theological ground on which they stand. Here begins the religious understanding of community and its benefits to the believer, its inclusion of the marginalized, and its connection to the God who creates human community and blesses it.

THEOLOGY AND COMMUNITY

The Bible is a book that tells of the many ways God has called believers into community. The characters of the stories therein are never in isolation from their communities of faith; moreover, they seem to seek out community with their people and with God. The fundamental community of the Bible is the nation of Israel and their relationship with God. Brueggemann (1997), professor emeritus of Old Testament at Columbia Theological Seminary, writes about the society of the people of Israel and especially how that society was impacted by the exile to Babylon. Who they became in exile was a model for human communities in general and faith communities in particular. Brueggemann describes four ways of being, which are as follow.

First, "the ancient community of the exiles learned to express sadness, rage, anger and loss honestly. . . . Ancient Israel broke the pattern of denial by engaging in speeches of complaint and lamentation" (p. 630). Second, "Ancient Israel also models for us the disciplines of order and holiness" and "these displaced people for whom almost everything was out of control set out to reorder and recover life through an intentional resolve about communion with God" (p. 631). Brueggemann points to Sabbath as the point around which life was reordered, recalling both the story of Creation and the covenant with Moses.

Third, the author cites the "striving to establish a sense of community." He writes that "the Deuteronomic tradition presents society as a neighborhood and enjoins attitudes and policies that enhance neighborliness . . . maintaining a public economy of compassion and justice is a way to move beyond despair" (p. 631). For Brueggemann, the idea of community stands over against the individualism and "dislocation" that work to divide people. In a time of crisis, preserving community meant survival in a foreign land. Fourth is "to proclaim the God who creates new social possibilities beyond the shrunken horizons of defeat and submissive docility . . . and the new social possibilities rooted in the truth of God's good news" (p. 632).

Brueggemann highlights a way of thinking about community that is central to the model of community care for the mentally ill advocated here. The powerful intent of this model is the community that is active in maintaining connections and values. For the client with psychiatric illness, this kind of community provides the secure environment that can tolerate expressions of pain, provide order to a chaotic mind, and offer holiness and transcendence as a new reality that offers a different way of healing.

As the people of Israel established community in the Old Testament, so did the early church create community in the New Testament. The wonderful depiction of the Christian community in Acts 2: 43-47 and 4:32-37 seems in line with the model of the people of

Israel. As Soelle (1985) has written for *Theology Today,* "Their slogan was not, 'God helps those who help themselves.' Rather, because God helps everyone, they were there to help each other. That is the church—or better yet, that is what the church should be; each one for everyone" (p. 216). As Soelle unpacks the idea of "having everything in common" she observes that one common element is the stories we share.

> Our own lives, isolated and separated from others, are barren and insufficient; we have therefore linked ourselves up with the desires, the courage, and the work of the many. . . . Church means also to have a place where such stories are remembered and told . . . when a person grows old in dignity, he then learns that it doesn't matter whether he has won every victory by himself alone. (pp. 218-219)

As Brueggemann interprets the community experience of the people of Israel, so Soelle does for the early church. Having everything in common carries a materialistic connotation, and rightfully so. Yet the deeper hermeneutic here is the meaning of lives that are lived together with a common story and an ever-present God. Her application of this understanding of community to the modern church is most meaningful. The community of the parish gives members and their pastor opportunity to tell their own individual stories and the stories of that congregation. What is healing for a congregation in time of trouble is the remembering of common stories that connect each to another. That is the enduring meaning of having all things in common.

Theologies of liberation hold the practice of community as central to the doctrine of salvation. Gustavo Gutierrez is the foremost teacher of soteriology as communal. Murray (1998) has researched extensively the doctrine of communal salvation in Gutierrez' work. She explains, "Community is the basis of Gutierrez' soteriology . . . human beings are called to meet God insofar as they constitute a community . . . we are saved within a liberative community engaged in transformative historical praxis among the marginalized" (p. 51).

It is Gutierrez's understanding of community beginning in God's love that directs us to a "commitment to the poor, in acts of solidarity freely chosen out of love, witnesses to a loving God who gratuitously seeks restored communion through justice for all" (p. 53).

Murray also finds in Gutierrez's work an exploration of spirituality, and it too is communal:

> The following of Jesus is not, purely or primarily, an individual matter but a collective adventure. . . . To recognize that the following of Jesus is undertaken along a communal route rather than along some private path is to recover the biblical understanding of the journey of a people in search of God, that is, of spirituality. (p. 55)

The practice of communal spirituality is in some ways difficult to envision, yet it is supported by every reference in the Bible to an experience of God. For the community to find its identity in the ways of Christ, it is called to formation and ministry on behalf of the poor and marginalized. In this way, liberation theology calls the communities of faith to work on behalf of the mentally ill, including them fully in their life and working as advocates for them in society.

Volf (1996), professor of theology at Yale Divinity School, uses different language to conceptualize the processes of community. He uses the phrase "grace to embrace" to refer to the Christian act of reconciliation. Since the formation of community must certainly require reconciliation, what Volf writes is pertinent to our discussion. In his book, *Exclusion and Embrace,* Volf addresses the issue of community:

> First, the grace of embrace must help justice deal adequately with ever-changing differences among human beings. The stability and universality of justice need to be kept flexible by mercy's sensitivity to the particularities of a given situation. (p. 224)
>
> But if we see human beings as children of the one God, created by God to belong all together as a community of love, then there will be good reasons to let embrace love define what justice is. (p. 225)

The healing of relationships is a concept vital to the theology of community. Volf offers the image of "embrace" in order to convey that concept more concretely and powerfully. Communities of compassion will embrace each member as a valued and loved part of the communal life. The "grace to embrace" implies giving up former relationships of power, and taking on relationships of inclusion and unconditional acceptance.

APPLYING SPIRITUALITY, COMMUNITY, AND PSYCHOTHERAPY

Griffith and Griffith (2002) contribute to the search for integration of community and spiritual experience in psychotherapy with their book *Encountering the Sacred in Psychotherapy*. The two most compelling ideas developed by the authors are the community as a "nurturing place" and the community as helping people to "remember."

The concept of place refers not only to a location but a structure in which our lives take place. For many this structure includes a spiritual community, in which beneficial relationships can develop and knit together a family of people for the purpose of living according to the ways of God. The authors write that one's place is where conversations could occur, from social greetings to mundane chatter to serious discussions. "Daily routines throughout the neighborhood gave a sense of order and expectation to the relatedness that had developed among the families . . . the sense of belonging, which is necessary for psychological well-being, depends on strong, well-developed relationships with nurturing places" (p. 193). The spiritual community creates a social reality that meets social needs, and at the same time heightens the meaning of social interaction from merely human relationship to sacred relationship. Because the community helps the person maintain religious practices and enacts sacramental experiences, the benefit becomes one of the constant presence of God within a group of people who believe that when they gather, God will indeed be present.

What the Griffiths present is critical for the practice of pastoral counseling. The client comes to the pastoral counselor because, consciously or unconsciously, he or she expects the therapy hour to take place in the presence of God. The gathering of therapist and client becomes a spiritual community. The counseling office becomes sacred space, and the structure of the counseling relationship enacts the presence of God by its very identity as something sacred. The holy nurturing that takes place in the counseling is the product of the pastoral counselor's spiritual community with the client. For the bipolar client, having a holy place to reveal struggles and find some peace in all the chaos is critically important. The pastoral counseling office may be the best place to find a sense of God-given order in life.

Subsequently, the Griffiths introduce a term from anthropology that they have found useful in the narrative context of therapy:

> Re-membering calls attention to the reaggregation of members, the figures who belong to one's life story, one's own prior selves, as well as significant others who are part of the story. Re-membering, then is a purposive, significant unification, quite different from the passive, continuous, fragmentary flickerings of images and feelings that accompany other activities in the normal flow of consciousness. (p. 209)

What this looks like in community was described eloquently by one of their clients, who found that her community helped her "re-member" herself into a new appreciation of her identity:

> I have friends who love me, here now, who can say to me the words I need to hear. Some I could have imagined, but some I needed to hear. So I asked them. You know, the wonderful thing was that they not only gave me their words of encouragement, but their presence. . . . I wrote their words down, too, so the anxiety could not make me forget them. (p. 210)

In this client's experience, the problems she carried with her actually "dis-membered" her by cutting her off from her communities of support and obscuring her sense of identity. The spiritual reality here is that our separation from God is just like that, and may be intricately woven together with our psychological experience of dis-memberment. If we feel we have no membership in society, then our personal sense of belonging to God is prone to wither as well. The person with bipolar disorder knows all too well the experience of being cut off from others by the illness and his or her actions. If the pastoral counselor can help that client re-member who she is and find new communities in which she is nurtured and given room to grow, then that client finds an identity he or she has not previously known, perhaps an identity that he or she has always known to be possible. This is the experience of joining with God in finding his or her God-given identity as a child of God's creation, who has been given a uniqueness that can be celebrated, not suffered.

The Griffiths end their study by suggesting some strategies for having open spiritual dialogue in therapy sessions. The one that seemed most appropriate for this study was "articulating religious beliefs in language evocative of hope and intimacy with God" (p. 296). Much of our religious language comes from the visual imagery in the Bible, and some of it may need reexamination in light of a client's identity issues. The male-dominant images of God learned from childhood may no longer be useful to a woman who has been abused by men her whole life. She may find the God images throughout Scripture of God as a maternal figure, caring for her young or nursing them on her breast more meaningful. For the bipolar client, images of God run rampant through the mental chaos most sufferers experience. Marianne was just such a woman, whose traditional God imagery was harmful to her. She sought a way to practice her spirituality in a more New Age form, and it served her well in reconnecting her to the Spirit that gave her life. Terry's practice of religion was in a traditional setting (Methodism), yet his internal faith was much more deeply rooted in the language of the twelve-step movement, as he called upon his Higher Power, and relying on this Higher Power for daily assistance in coping with sobriety. Once again, God's nurturing power was much more evident in Terry's life than God's judgment or fatherhood. God as father would not have been a workable model for a man whose father had so disregarded Terry's humanity as a child.

So much of our religious experience in community is influenced by our use of language. Pastoral counselors are challenged to help their clients find language that will support them in their struggles and find a way to experience God that gives them wholeness and healing. The languages of a number of spiritual communities are available as resources for therapists in their work with suffering people. Creating a healing spiritual community in the counseling office and outside in the client's personal world can reconnect people to their identities as children of God, and their place in God's creation.

Chapter 6

Theological Reflection on Bipolar Disorder

Above all, trust in the slow work of God.

Pierre Teilhard de Chardin (1999)

In this chapter, the focus narrows to the theological meanings and expressions that might help a person with bipolar disorder find connection to God and faith, defined here as a theology of relatedness. The theology of Edward Schillebeeckx, a twentieth-century Dominican scholar, speaks most directly to the problems of believing in God when faced with an endless experience of mental anguish. This chapter will highlight two of the teachings of Schillebeeckx, his doctrine of suffering and his understanding of freedom and solidarity. Within each rubric will be reflection on how the claims made by the author will illuminate an image of God, the dialogue with pastoral counseling, and the application to bipolar disorder. The choice is made here to explore the response of Christian faith to mental illness, as it is my own faith tradition, and the one in which I have found meaning for this struggle. This study has demonstrated a variety of spiritual approaches and, I hope, has honored those which are not my own. I choose to use Christian theology here for my ongoing dialogue with my own faith, and because I believe that Christian theology speaks to the hopes for relatedness in human society. If the teachings of Jesus are in any way relevant to us in the twenty-first century, they are so in their call to relationships of wholeness and unconditional love.

The Treatment of Bipolar Disorder in Pastoral Counseling

doi:10.1300/5696_07

SUFFERING IN SCHILLEBEECKX'S THEOLOGY

McManus (1999, pp. 476-491) published a study of the theologian's thinking on the problem of suffering, which will help the concise presentation of this chapter. Schillebeeckx reflected on the nature of suffering in a dialectical fashion, namely, that because suffering is a part of human experience, it must always be understood in partnership with hope and the promises of God. McManus writes that "Suffering constitutes the raw and immediate challenge to countless concrete lives running desperately short of expectation . . . the cause of affliction may be internal or external . . . suffering (has) physical, psychic and spiritual dimensions" (p. 476). For Schillebeeckx, suffering must be understood by theology in the "narrative structure of experience" in which is the "incarnational view of the human person who participates in the divinely created order." One such story is the one

> hidden away in middle class homes and behind the polished facades of the affluent. The immediacy of loneliness, the rawness of broken relationships, the incomprehensible pain of mental illness, the dearth of hope when the fulfillment of our desires leaves emptiness unassuaged, the slow relinquishing of life with age. (p. 477)

In various ways, Schillebeeckx draws the action of God into this reflection, especially in the image of "God As Liberator" who brings freedom to those who have been oppressed. Also, he reflects on the person of Jesus in the suffering of humanity and its salvation. The relational nature of Jesus is the central theological theme here, and Christ is portrayed as being in complete solidarity with those who suffer. McManus calls this a "relational ontology" and makes the dialectical interpretation of the simultaneous communion with humanity of Jesus and the communion Jesus had with God. "In the light of Jesus Christ, the gospel itself is a hermeneutic of humanity from which we must interpret the gospel, and vice versa" (p. 478). Since the experience of Jesus in the Gospels has as its central element his suffering and death for humanity, Jesus walks in solidarity with all those who are enslaved in body or mind. God through Christ is then in solidarity with each person as their Creator.

The idea of solidarity extends further in Schillebeeckx's work on community and suffering. The central symbol here is the cross,

> experienced in each personal turning or *metanoia* which does not take place outside of history or apart from one's social, communal situatedness but in the depths of the human heart. . . . By mysterious twists and turns, the reality of suffering illumines the paradoxical truth of our human existence: uniquely solitary in personhood before God, yet created for community, structured as mediators of grace for one another. (p. 481)

Schillebeeckx has created a dialectical concept of human suffering fortified by belief in a God who is for us completely, through the Son, Jesus Christ. The God who loves us understands our suffering and seeks to save us from it. Not only does God sympathize; God walks in solidarity with all who suffer, as God himself walked on the earth in the person of Jesus Christ. This idea opposes doctrines of suffering which assign a root cause in human actions. In traditional theologies of retribution, God punishes the sinner with suffering until payment is exacted. Schillebeeckx looks back to the theology of Saint Thomas Aquinas for a perspective that sees the presence of evil in the world as totally opposed to God's purposes. God stands against all forms of evil and only for the hope that evil will be overcome.

This theology also has a strong communal component, which brings the experience of suffering out of hiding and into view of the community where healing and hope may be found. For many, God is a being who is the Other, whom one can never really know. In a theology of community, God is known by our knowledge of Jesus Christ, and by the acts of Christlike love that happen between members of the community. Solidarity in community means people of all types who have suffered in their own ways offering that knowledge of suffering to the group for the edification of all. Those who have endured suffering and emerged with a stronger faith may be in ministry to those who currently suffer and cannot believe. Remembering the "hermeneutic of humanity," one may see the truth of the Gospel being lived out in the lives of members of the community and taught to those who suffer.

Certainly Schillebeeckx offers a pastoral theology that guides the pastoral counselor in reflecting on clients' experience and seeing theological themes in the counseling relationship. One component of pastoral counseling involves the working through of the experiences of life and finding in them ways to see God at work, and to discern meaning in painful experiences. Schillebeeckx formulates an understanding of suffering that validates the pain of the sufferer and affirms the goodness of God in the face of brokenness. When a client can integrate an open acceptance of suffering and acknowledge the goodness and present help of God, then he has begun to move toward health and away from bitterness.

Another root problem in the pastoral counseling office is the sense the client often has of being completely alone in his or her troubles. The societal context reinforces the idea of being alone with one's problems, and affirms the value of handling one's own problems by one's self. The message of the gospels could not be any more different. Christ came into the world to establish solidarity with the people. Any problem can be brought to another person and the burden shared. Schillebeeckx outlines a strong doctrine of suffering in community, undergirded by the notion that full humanity is achieved through relationality. The incarnation of Christ did not happen in a vacuum; it involved the community of Israel and in it God affirmed the connectedness between humanity and the divine life. Schillebeeckx's dialectical understanding of sin and suffering, creation and salvation, offers us a perspective in the counseling situation that may bring balance and integration to someone dealing with the paradoxes of life.

Of what value might Schillebeeckx's theology be to the bipolar client? McManus describes his theology of suffering as mystical. This resonates with the inner experience of manic-depressive people. To them, their disease is a mystery, and the treatment even more mysterious. They don't know why they behave the way they do, they can't explain the racing internal thoughts and chaos, and they cannot trace the origins of the illness to any one cause. Coming to terms with all of these unknowns involves a quest for the meaning of the illness and an informed approach to its treatment and cure. Schillebeeckx's writing shows a well-developed incarnational theology that bridges the gap between mysticism and experience. Suffering is still a mystery; even Jesus struggles with it, all the way to the cross. But the more unfathomable mystery is why God would come down to humanity and enter into their suffering. This is the beginning point for finding meaning in a life full of suffering. Bipolar sufferers daily reexperiences an inner madness that is unbearable. Even with medication, they have breakthroughs of psychotic symptoms and periods of depression. The side effects of the medications can be debilitating, and the changes in work and family life can be disruptive. If the client experiences God's companionship, then the sense of isolation begins to diminish. The company of Christ brings the desire to reconnect with the community of faith, which in turn can nurture the person toward new life in a group that accepts them without condition.

Bipolar clients may sense that what they experience is an expression of evil. The kind of thoughts and the varieties of behaviors they engage in are not what a rational person would think or do. The client knows this, and thus wrestles with the notion that they may have a force within them they cannot control. In a theological sense, the evil cannot be fully understood. Schillebeeckx defined this as the "negative contrast experience." What can be grasped is the way God stands against the evil and for the person and his or her salvation. The promise of solidarity with God when one's self-image is that of an evil person is revolutionary in one's spiritual life. The God who would stand with the sinner and advocate for his or her restoration to the community is the God of grace who came in Jesus Christ.

SOLIDARITY AND FREEDOM

Alongside the doctrine of suffering lies the doctrine of freedom, a freedom that, in Schillebeeckx' theology, always includes God's solidarity. McManus describes it this way:

> It has different manifestations in accord with the vastly different types of individual and communal suffering. The praxis of solidarity is manifest in transformative action as well as resistance and protest. In situations of extreme suffering, it appears as faithful waiting: attentive love in a "now" that belies the promise that sustains us. The praxis of solidarity is a contemplative, relational praxis, demanding the hard work of reconciliation together with the paradoxical knowing that reconciliation is a gift of grace. (p. 490)

Paired with the idea of transformative action is that of the "discipleship of presence," where the sufferer is met by friends who are "still free to act in hope or wait in the fruitful silence of reverent solidarity" (p. 482). Sometimes human suffering leaves us without words; but this does not preclude an act of solidarity by a fellow traveler that restores one's relation to the community of faith. The tolerance of silence brings all to an admission of their dependence on God to end suffering and create wholeness again. Not only is silence a human expression of community; it is a reminder of the intimacy of Christ with us that declares the temporary nature of suffering:

> The crisis of meaning and faith enters in when the praxis of justice is thwarted, and more critically, when radical, gratuitous suffering renders the presence of evil more evident and potent in the world than the presence of God or goodness. At the place where human effort or understanding reaches its limit and where God seems absent, there is evoked a praxis of solidarity. . . . The praxis of solidarity is rooted in Jesus' intimacy with God that sustained the cross and issued in his Resurrection. It is manifest in hopeless situations by the courageous, ministering human presence that alone witnesses to God's final word over suffering, sin and death. (p. 481)

The commitment to community in this theology and the incorporation of the ministry of presence provides a pastoral element. The human response to the suffering of another does not have to be impotent wordlessness. The shared knowledge of suffering and the common story of Jesus' suffering provides the words to the experience, even when silence is the best way of caring. In the face of human suffering, words about God only create hostility. A witness of presence to the one in pain tells the story of God's presence without words. Such a witness can be understood as a more powerful telling of the story. The witness of presence and silence tells of a God who walked through the wilderness with the people of Israel and walked with Jesus as he suffered and died on the cross. The change in our relationship to God happens in our realization of God's desire to be with us in the hardships of life, and the readiness of God toward establishing community with us at any time.

Once again, we see a direct application to the pastoral counseling setting. The client who comes for pastoral counseling is often undergoing a crisis of meaning in his or her life. The crisis may stem from an experience of suffering by the client or a family member. His or her existential problem appears to be, "How can I believe in a loving God when I have unmerited suffering?" The expressed problem contains the two underlying problems of the powerlessness of God and the presence of evil. So much is on the table when a client presents in this way. The temptation is for the counselor to answer all of the questions right away so that therapy might begin. Schillebeeckx's theology invites the counselor to permit the anxiety for awhile and allow the problem to first be faced in silence. This allows the client to be aware of the safe presence of the therapist and the permission to express difficult feelings. If the therapist is able to maintain a loving presence, then the client may begin to examine the experience internally. Then the exploration of suffering can happen in the "community of two" that has been forming. It may take some courage for the counselor to sit quietly for awhile, but once the client has understood the purpose of the counselor's silence, the concept of waiting together will become a central part of a deeper therapy and a solidarity of healing.

Applied to the treatment of bipolar disorder, the practice of a solidarity that issues in freedom is what clients most desire. They do not need talk; they have plenty of internal conversation already. What they require is an honest look at the suffering brought on by their illness and how it has kept them apart from God and their friends and family. As has already been demonstrated, the use of silence in therapy has a tremendous benefit to the client. Bipolar disorder creates an isolation from others that cannot be overcome by well-meaning friends or professionals. Only the solidarity of Christ in the witness of fellow believers can break down barriers and establish a connection.

A final concept to consider is the meaning of freedom in this context. In manic depression, one is a prisoner to wide mood swings and psychotic hallucinations. Even after treatment begins, the captivity to medications and their side effects creates a secondary problem that seems to be a never-ending story. The solidarity of Christ and its expression in the community of faith may be the only source of freedom for the client. It is in the community that suffering is fully accepted and understood, that the feelings can be openly expressed and accepted, that one is affirmed as a whole human being who happens to have an illness, and that the presence of Christ is always assured, in the religious expressions of worship and the community expressions of unconditional love. Freedom in this context becomes the freedom to be a part of the community that nurtures and supports the freedom to be fully human in the light of Christ.

CASE ANALYSIS

In analyzing the case in Chapter 5 using the theological reflections of Schillebeeckx, one begins with the experience of isolation. Terry was set apart from his community in many ways. In his earliest childhood experiences, he was denied a normal childhood and forced to function in an adult sexual role that excluded him from friendships and normal emotional and sexual development. His alcoholism caused many friends and family to withdraw from him and withhold love and care. His bipolar disorder drove him to extremes of impulsive behavior that eventually brought legal trouble. His wife and children, miraculously, stayed with Terry through the best and worst of all this.

In his internal life, Terry was troubled by manic episodes that fueled binges of sex, gambling, and stealing. The kind of mental chaos and loss of control that he experienced can only be imagined, yet all of the social acting out was really a cover for a feeling of complete isolation from others. Terry's suffering included the emptiness and loneliness that issued in behavior that, ironically, only created more of the same. Even with proper medications for bipolar illness, he continued to experience episodes of depression that caused absenteeism from work and periods of mania and psychosis that drove him to seek counseling.

According to Schillebeeckx' model, Terry experienced the depth of suffering in his spirit that only the practice of presence could address. No words would have helped Terry heal from a lifetime of mistreatment by others and self-induced abuse. The needs expressed by Terry were for relief from symptoms, certainly, but also for a reconnection with God and a sense of a Higher Power that could heal a profound mental illness. If God were to intervene in this life, it would happen incarnationally and in solidarity. Christ would be incarnate in the counseling relationship, embracing Terry with unconditional love and allowing him to be truly honest in the telling of his story and the unearthing of his feelings. Christ would be in solidarity with Terry by sharing in the experience of rejection and abuse. What Terry suffered was not unlike what Christ suffered, and suffered for him.

Finally, what this theological model offered was a concept of freedom that differed from a human idea of freedom. The kind of freedom offered to Terry in this situation was a freedom for a relationship with God that had nothing to do with merit or goodness or moral judgment. Freedom with God meant an intimacy with God such as that of

God with Christ on the cross. Christ could suffer as he did, feel abandoned and yet still have intimacy with God that sustained him through the most horrible way of dying imaginable. For Terry, freedom meant talking about the suffering openly, sitting silently and exploring the depths of his abandonment, and then beginning to build a new image of self that included his God-given creative abilities, which were many. A major loss was the news that Terry would be going to prison, for it ended a relationship that I had come to value and learn from. Prison would be a rough road for Terry, and I could not help him. I could only pray that the work that had begun in my office could continue safely somewhere else. I prayed also for Terry's life as a sex offender in a brutal state prison. If he could survive this experience and find community within the prison walls, then he could return to his family and have a chance at happiness.

Chapter 7

Conclusions

What are the ways in which this book contributes to the clinical understanding and treatment of bipolar clients in pastoral counseling? What are the methods that seem most effective and inform the practice of pastoral counseling with the mentally ill? This final chapter will bring out the ideas from each chapter that are informative to the counselor and may advance the psychological and theological understanding of practitioners.

The school of psychotherapy that seems most transferable to pastoral counseling is family systems. The idea of changing the system for the good of the patient and treating the patient within the context of all his various systems—family, community, and world—is a familiar one for pastors and pastoral counselors. For clients with bipolar disorder, dysfunctional systems have supported their pathology and resisted change that would help the client. Pastoral counseling takes as its method a holistic approach rather than an individual one. Therefore, the family psychoeducation theory and the structural method of family therapy each offer the family a chance to change the ways in which they interact for the good of the client whom they have identified as the "sick one." Also operating in the systems realm is the narrative approach to family therapy, a way of doing psychotherapy that assists the family members to tell their common story and make connections with one another based on that story. In this context, the client gets to tell his or her version and work toward a vision of the story that reconciles the illness with his or her family problems. In all these ways, pastoral counselors, who are skilled at congregational dynamics, can bring the same insight to the troubled family. For persons with bipolar disorder, being reconnected to their families and sources of support can happen in the framework of family therapy.

The Treatment of Bipolar Disorder in Pastoral Counseling

doi:10.1300/5696_08

Pastoral counseling theory has placed one of its emphases on the centrality of community in the healing process. This book has addressed the contributions of pastoral theologians who recognize the value of community in changing unhealthy ways and creating new patterns of wholeness. Clinebell defined the church as a nurturing community of growth. Patton argued for a model of relational humanness in the practice of pastoral counseling. Hunter stressed the importance of church-centered counseling for the practice of pastoral counseling. Ashbrook expanded the community to include an interdependence with the practice of medicine on behalf of mentally ill clients. Graham recognized the theological themes inherent in family therapy and argued for the necessity of this method of counseling in the pastoral counseling office. In each of these opinions, pastoral counselors are urged to take on a practice of systemic therapy that includes the context of clients who may only see themselves as isolated individuals. What happens when the system is recognized is a dramatic shift in the locus of change, and a mobilization of community resources on behalf of the client. Isolation then diminishes and connectedness increases. Connectedness is defined by the biblical notion of the community of faith, inspired by God's Spirit.

Supporting the work of pastoral theologians have been those who engage in the dialogue between religion and science, seeking mutual understanding and informing one another's practices. Leading the movement toward shared research has been Benson, who has studied the link between mind and body and the effect of mental states on physical functioning. His findings on the positive effects of centering prayer on heart rate and blood pressure give hope to all who make meditation part of their counseling. Specifically for pastoral counselors, the use of centering prayer is another avenue to relating faith to the problems of life, and a mode of treatment for more severe mental disturbance. If the benefits of prayer are physical as well as spiritual, then the use of prayer in counseling can be not only cognitive or behavioral, but biological as well.

Also in the science and religion discussion belongs the study of sociologists who seek to find the possible benefits of the faith community on a person's health and well-being. The studies cited in this paper bear out the hypothesis that active participation in a faith community can improve mental health. For pastoral counselors this provides solid evidence for encouraging faith-group membership for clients. If healing takes place in a caring group of believers, then the counselor is justified in helping the client find an appropriate faith community. The practice of pastoral counseling in the parish setting is supported by these findings. The presence of a congregational commitment to pastoral counseling becomes part of the healing process.

The principles of Quakerism informed our discussion of care for the psychiatric patient. In both their historical expression and current practice, the Quakers have set a standard for humane care for the mentally ill that is unrivaled. Moreover, the foundational ideas upon which this care is based are relevant to the efforts of pastoral counselors to give care to the mentally ill. These fundamentals include acceptance of the patient into the community as a whole person created by God, fostering self-worth and a fully human image of the self, assisting nature in healing by creating a proper environment, and providing social contact that promotes healing and eliminates isolation. Also, the Quaker ideal includes the responsibility of patients for their public behavior, and the practice of silence in worship that reconnects one to the light of Christ within.

These principles are highly relevant to the practice of pastoral counseling. In particular, they are relevant to the task of assisting the mentally ill toward health and restoration to society. To incorporate these into one's practice of pastoral counseling would involve two steps. First would be to include them in an overall philosophy of pastoral counseling that seeks to find within clients a spark of light and life, and an image of self as a whole person made in the likeness of God. This philosophy would counteract any tendency to focus on pathology, or to see clients merely as poorly functioning, incomplete people. Here again is where systems theory contributes a view of clients as part of a larger, pathological system, and seeks to help them discover their strengths and change their roles in the system. Pathologizing may be important for the medical diagnosis, but it may be more productive for clients to see themselves not as inadequate or incomplete, but as persons in need of change in a system that also needs change.

Second, incorporating Quaker beliefs into pastoral counseling could include establishing a practice of silence in the therapy hour that facilitates a process of internal reconnection. Pastoral counseling models that rely exclusively on talk and personal analysis of thoughts and behavior don't allow the deeper experience of emotions and the remembering of past trauma and previous relationships. The use of silence in therapy must be intentional and directed, yet must also allow for the client to discover things about himself that the therapist could not know. Therefore, giving time for quieting the mind, for allowing feelings and memories to arise, and for encouraging the client to verbalize these experiences may be at least as valuable as talking and interpreting. In my own experience this was very true; without the time in silence I would not have connected to long-lost memories and emotions. Pastoral counseling's unique place in the mental health professions involves the exploration of spiritual experience and deep meaning. Silence can clear the pathway into both places.

The review of the use of silence in psychotherapy yielded some crucial insights into the nature of the time spent in silence and its therapeutic value. Many writers agreed that the practice of centering prayer allows an encounter between God and the self. What they differed on was what actually happens while this encounter is taking place. Some saw the silence as being in a dialectic with speech, as part of an interplay of activities. Others saw the practice of silence as relational, happening always in the context of relationship that permits mutual presence without conversation. In this view, the relational nature of silence is what can bring healing to the troubled inner spirit. Still another way of understanding silence was as the cultivation of a state of mindfulness, an attitude of prayer that fosters attention to the inner working of the self and the ways that God is working within the self. This is a Buddhist concept widely practiced in both the East and West. The Christian parallel to this concept is self-emptying, a concept the origin of which was in Christ's emptying of himself on the cross for our benefit. The believer in this context seeks to imitate a sacrificial way of life and empty himself or herself of needs and wants that get in the way of an open relationship with God.

In the pastoral counseling relationship, the choice of whether or how to use silence will depend on the needs of the client and his or her level of comfort with spiritual practices. Terry was accustomed to the language of Alcoholics Anonymous, and could easily embrace the self-emptying approach to prayer and therapy. For my own treatment, the use of silence included both the interplay of silence and speech, and the relationality of silence I felt with Michael. Whichever method is chosen, a sense of mutuality must be established before the therapist can suggest a way of spiritual practice. If the client participates in the choice of silent practice, he can embrace it more fully and reap the full benefit.

This book culminates with the singular role of community in helping a person to find wholeness and healing. In the practical realm, it has been shown that community can provide fullness of life that reverses a move toward isolation and despair. In religious communities, beliefs and rituals may keep the numbers of members who relapse into drug abuse or suicide much lower than normal. The community that can fully integrate its members, including the mentally ill, becomes that expression of the Body of Christ that was the work of the New Testament church. Along these lines, the biblical models in the Old Testament of the people of Israel and their walk with God show a community that provided order and holiness to its members, and allowed them to overcome tremendous odds in returning from exile in Babylon and re-create a just society. The vibrant exposition of the liberation theologians, of the doctrines of communal spirituality and the sacramental place of the community in the work of God, brings the experience of modern Christians together again with the people of Israel. The metaphor of liberation from slavery, applied to contemporary social injustice, provides a clear pointer to the work of Christ that is still to be done in the world.

For the pastoral counselor, the work toward community is in two parts. First is the establishment of community with the client in the therapy office. Jesus gave the model of "wherever two or three are gathered" for pastoral counselors as well. Community in this context means a place where the client can be fully himself or herself and be accepted. It means an environment that holds him or her safely and allows the expression of the negative parts of the self that are not welcomed in any other place. It means a reciprocal relationship with the therapist that promises honest response spoken lovingly.

Second, the pastoral counselor practices in a church-sponsored environment where the client knows that he or she has entered a community of grace, a community where God is present. This may be the most meaningful aspect of the pastoral counselor's place in the therapeutic world. Wherever the counselor is, the blessing of the church follows him or her in his or her ordination, and the blessing extends to the clients in his or her office. In the Old Testament sense, he or she is the priest who points the people to the pillar of cloud and fire and invites them to come along on the journey. The counseling relationship becomes a place of order and holiness. In a New Testament sense, the client becomes a part of the Body of Christ, where Christ's presence is experienced anew and the self is a new creation.

Bipolar disorder is a severe mental illness that creates wide gulfs between a person and his or her true self, and a person and the community. The pastoral counselor offers guidance in bridging these gulfs, and encourages the spiritual journey of healing. The practices of silence and community offer the bipolar client the best chance to find peace from his or her inner turmoil and reconciliation with those he or she has alienated. Neither of these practices are familiar or comfortable to most clients. The pastoral counselor invites them into new patterns of relationship with God, self, and others. Transformation and healing occur under such conditions. Pastoral counselors can provide the safe context in which these potentials are realized in the lives of real people.

References

Chapter 1

Angst, F. (2002). High suicide rates among patients with mood disorders. *Journal of Affective Disorders, 68,* 167-181.

Barondes, S. (1998). *Mood Genes: Hunting for Origins of Mania and Depression.* New York: W. H. Freeman.

Berzoff, J., Flanagan, L.M., and Hertz, P. (1996). *Inside Out and Outside In.* Northvale, NJ: Jason Aronson Inc.

Egeland, J., Hostetter, A., Pauls, D., and Sussex, J. (2000). Prodromal symptoms before onset of manic-depressive disorder suggested by first hospital admission histories. *Journal of the American Academy of Child and Adolescent Psychiatry, 39,* 10.

Electroconvulsive Therapy (2001, January). *American Healthline, 7.*

Fishbane, M. (2001). Relational narratives of the self. *Family Process, 40,* 273-291.

Frank, E. (2001). Managing bipolar depression. 154th Meeting of the American Psychiatric Association, New Orleans.

Freud, S. (1905). A case of hysteria. *Standard Edition, 3,* 191-225.

Friedrich, M. (1999). Lithium: Proving its mettle for 50 years. *Journal of the American Medical Association, 281:*24, 2271.

Goodman, H. (2001). Genetic study of schizophrenia/bipolar disorder initiated. *Psychiatry Matters.* Available at www.psychiatrymatters.md.

Griswold, K. and Pessar, L. (2000). The management of bipolar disorder. *American Family Physician, 62,* 1343-1358.

Himmelhoch, J. and Thase, M. (1994). General clinical approach to bipolar patients. *First International Conference on Bipolar Disorder.* Available at www.mentalhealth.com.

Hirschfeld, R. (2002). New bipolar treatment guideline from APA. *Mental Health Weekly, 12:*17, 1.

Jamison, K. (1995). *An Unquiet Mind.* New York: Vintage Books.

Johnson, B. (2001). Electroconvulsive treatment. *Consultant Psychiatric Review,* December 19, 5.

Kerr, M. and Bowen, M. (1988). *Family Evaluation.* New York: W.W. Norton.

Kestenbaum, C. (2000). How shall we treat children in the 21st century? *Journal of the American Academy of Child and Adolescent Psychiatry, 39,* 5.

doi:10.1300/5696_09

Kimberly. (2002). Severe depression relieved. *Integrated Healthcare*. Available at www.ecopolitan.com/ihe/severedepression.html.

Klein, M. (1957). *Envy and Gratitude*. New York: Free Press.

Kraus, A. (1995). Psychotherapy based in identity problems of depressives. *American Journal of Psychotherapy, 49,* 197-212.

Kugler, P. (1994). Clinical Psychopathology. Available at cgjungpage.org.

Kupfer, D. (1994). Clinical approaches and guidelines for treatment. Report on 1st International Conference on Bipolar Disorder, Pittsburgh.

Laroi, F. (2000). Treating families of individuals with traumatic brain injury. *Journal of Family Psychotherapy, 11:*4, 69-77.

Lerer, K. (2000). Twirling in space: My experience with shock therapy. *Psychology Today, 32:*3, 28.

Lewis, R. (1996). Evening out the ups and downs of manic depressive illness. *FDA Consumer, 30.*

MacKinnon, R. and Michels, R. (1971). *The Psychiatric Interview in Clinical Practice*. Philadelphia: W.B. Saunders Company.

Mahony, E. (2002). Sibling study of bipolar disorder. *Psychological Medicine, 32,* 55-61.

Mallinger, A. (1994). Polypharmacy and the treatment of bipolar disorder. *First International Conference on Bipolar Disorder*. Available at www.mentalhealth.com.

McWilliams, N. (1994). *Psychoanalytic Diagnosis*. New York: Guilford Press.

Miklowitz, D. and Goldstein, M. (1997). *Bipolar Disorder: A Family-Focused Treatment Approach*. New York: Guilford Press.

Minerd, J. (1999). The hunt for mood genes. *The Futurist, 5:*11.

Patten-Hitt, E. (2001). Psychobiology and psychopharmacotherapy. Report on 154th Meeting of the American Psychiatric Association, New Orleans.

Petersen, C. (2000). Second-generation drugs and combo therapy improve BPD outlook. *Managed Healthcare, 10:*8, 45-46.

Racker, H. (1968). *Transference and Countertransference*. Madison, CT: International Universities Press.

Reidel, H., Heiby, E., and Kopetskie, S. (2001). Psychological behaviorism theory of bipolar disorder. *The Psychological Record, 51,* 507-532.

Rosenfarb, I. (2001). Family transactions and relapse in bipolar disorder. *Family Process, 40,* 5-14.

Strobel, M. (2000). The genetics of behavioral traits. *The Hastings Center Report, 30,* 4-47.

Ten Have, M. (2002). Bipolar patients fail to seek help for their condition. *Journal of Affective Disorders, 68,* 203-213.

The Novel Antipsychotic Drugs. (2002, September). *Harvard Mental Health Letter, 19:*3, 5.

Tompson, M. (2000). Difficulty in implementing a family intervention for bipolar disorder. *Family Process, 39,* 105-120.

Wals, E., Hillegers, M., Reichart, C., Ormel, J., Nolen, W., and Verhulst, F. (2001). Prevalence of psychopathology in children of bipolar parent. *Journal of the American Academy of Child and Adolescent Psychiatry, 40:*9, 1094-1102.

Young, A. (2000). Treatment of bipolar affective disorder: New drug treatments. *British Medical Journal*, November 25.

Chapter 2

Ashbrook, J. (1988). *Paul Tillich in Conversation*. Bristol, IN: Wyndham Hall Press.

Ashbrook, J. (1994). Psychopharmacology and pastoral counseling: Medication and meaning. *The Journal of Pastoral Care, 49:*1, 5-18.

Ashbrook, J. and Albright, C. (1998). *The Humanizing Brain: Where Religion and Neuroscience Meet*. New York: Pilgrim Press.

Barshinger, C., Larowe, L., and Tapia, A. (1995). The gospel according to Prozac. *Christianity Today, 39*, 34-37.

Bass, E. and Davis, L. (1994). *The Courage to Heal*. New York: HarperCollins.

Capps, D. (2001). Curing anxious adolescents through fatherlike performance. *Interpretation, 55:*2, 135-147.

Clinebell, H. (1972). *The Mental Health Ministry of the Local Church*. Nashville, TN: Abingdon Press.

Faiver, C., O'Brien, E., and Ingersoll, R. (2000). Religion, guilt and mental health. *Journal of Counseling and Development, 78:*2, 155-161.

Graham, L. (1992). From psyche to system. *Theology Today, 49:*3, 320-332.

Hiltner, S. (1972). *Theological Dynamics*. Nashville, TN: Abingdon Press.

Hiltner, S. (1975). The outlook for mental health services. *The Christian Century*, October 29, 965-970.

Hunter, R. (2001). Spiritual counsel: An art in transition. *The Christian Century*, October 17, 20-25.

Jones, S. (1995). My genes made me do it. *Christianity Today, 39*, 14-18.

Kilpatrick, W. (1999). Faith and therapy. *First Things, 90*, 21-26.

Lacan, J. (1964). *The Four Fundamental Concepts of Psychoanalysis*. New York: W.W. Norton.

Lupton, J. (2000). Religion and psychoanalysis: Three fundamental concepts. *Journal for Culture and Religious Theory, 2:*1.

May, G. (1982). *Care of Mind, Care of Spirit*. San Francisco: Harper & Row.

McMillin, D. (1991). *The Treatment of Depression*. Virginia Beach: Meridian Institute.

Meier, A. (1997). The treatment of a major depressive episode using a pastoral counseling approach. *American Journal of Pastoral Counseling, 1:*1, 3-32.

Monteleone, R. (1997). The integrity of a narrative path: Circles of possibilities. *Journal of Pastoral Counseling, 32*.

Monteleone, R. (1999). Voice, support and strategy. *Journal of Pastoral Counseling, 34*.

O'Connell, R. (2001). The church and psychiatry. *America, 3*, 15-17.

O'Connor, M. (2002). Spiritual dark night and psychological depression. *Counseling and Values, 46:*2, 137-148.

Patton, J. (1981). Pastoral counseling comes of age. *The Christian Century,* March 4, 229-231.

Peterson, G. (1999). God on the brain: The neurobiology of faith. *The Christian Century, 116:*3, 84-88.

Savage, A. (2001). Pastoral theology/practice and Alfred Adler's individual psychology. *Quodlibet Online Journal of Christian Theology and Philosophy, 3:*3. Available at quodlibet.net.

Tillich, P. (1956). Address to the National Conference on Clinical Pastoral Education, Atlantic City, NJ. Available at www.acpe.edu.

Chapter 3

Amoss, G. (1988). Contemplation and freedom. *Journal of George Amoss.* Available at www.qia.net.

Amoss, G. (1995). Members of one body. *Journal of George Amoss.* Available at qis.net/-daruma/amoss.

Anderson, G. (2000). Of many things. *America, 183:*4.

Atta, K. and Roby, D. (1980). The Early Years of Friends Asylum 1817-1820. Available at friendshospital.org.

Bradstock, K. (2002). *Discovering a Quaker Theology of Pastoral Care.* Unpublished masters thesis, Wake Forest University, Winston-Salem, NC.

Damiano, K. (2002). Some Thoughts on Silence. Tract Association of Friends. Available at quakerinfo.com/silence.

Goerke, E. (1964). The Gift of Healing in the Life of George Fox. Available at quakerInfo.com.

Herman, M. (2002). Quakerdale's History. Available at www.quakerdale.org.

Quakers and Jungian Psychology. (1993). *Round Table Review.* Available at tcrp .quaker.org.

Reich, Max. (2002). *Congregational Silence.* Tract Association of Friends. Available at www.tractassociation.org.

Robinson, B. (2001). Religious Society of Friends. Available at religioustolerance .org/quaker.htm.

Roby, D. (1982). Pioneer of Moral Treatment: Isaac Bonsall. Available at friendshospital.org.

Samuel, B. (2001). Spiritual Silence in the Experience of Friends (Quakers). Available at quakerinfo.com/quaksil.shtml.

Wallis, J. (1992). *Jung and the Quaker Way.* London: Quaker Home Service.

Weening, H. (2002). *Meeting the Spirit.* Available at quaker.org/fwcc.

Whitaker, R. (2002). *Mad in America.* Cambridge: Perseus Publishing.

White, Z. (1998). *A Quaker Theology of Pastoral Care: The Art of the Everyday.* Wallingford, PA: Pendle Hill.

Chapter 4

Benson, H. (1975). *The Relaxation Response.* New York: HarperCollins.

Benson, H. (1996). Mindful healing: An interview. *Technology Review, 99*, 33-40.

Bogart, G. (1991). Meditation and psychotherapy: A review of the literature. *The American Journal of Psychotherapy, 45:*1.

Brown, C. (1999). Can Buddhism save? *Cross Currents, 49:*2, 164-196.

Burns, D. (2002). Buddhist meditation and depth psychology. *Psychotherapy, Meditation and Spirituality.* Available at www.buddhanet.net.

Cistercian Nuns of Santa Rita Abbey. (2002). Silence, Prayer, Liturgy. Available at santaritabbey.org.

Culligan, K. (1996). Spirituality and healing in medicine. *America, 175,* 17-21.

Epstein, M. (1998). Therapy and meditation: A path to wholeness. *Psychology Today, 31.*

Friedland, J. (1999). Compassion as a means to freedom. *The Humanist, 59:*4, 35-39.

Guenther, M. (1995). Embracing the silence. *The Christian Century, 112,* 603.

Jonas, R. (2002). A Dialogue with the Dalai Lama. The World Community for Christian Meditation. Available at www.theemptybell.org.

Kolin, P. (2001). Jeweled silence. *Christianity and Literature, 50:*2.

Lane, B. (1989). Merton as Zen clown. *Theology Today, 46:*3, 256-264.

Lew, A. (2000). Prayer and the uses of meditation. *Judaism, 49:*1, 93-101.

Lounibos, J. (2000). Self-emptying in Christian and Buddhist spirituality. *Journal of Pastoral Counseling, 35,* 49-66.

Powell, W. (2001). On creating a space: An interview with Parker Palmer. *Families in Society, 82:*1, 13-22.

Redmont, J. (1995). Praying in a time of depression. *America, 173,* 14-20.

Sandman, J. (2000). Centering prayer: A treasure for the soul. *America, 183:*6, 12-14.

Shealy, S. (2002a). Mindfulness: Taming a wild horse. *Buddhist Review.* Available at steveshealyphd.com.

Shealy, S. (2002b). Riding the dragon: The dance between psychotherapy and meditation. *Buddhist Review.* Available at steveshealyphd.com.

Wang, Y. (2001). Liberating oneself from the absolutized boundary of language. *Philosophy East and West, 51:*1, 83-99.

Chapter 5

Agarwal, M., Sharma, V., Kumar, K., and Lowe, D. (1998). Non-compliance with treatment in patients suffering from schizophrenia. *International Journal of Social Psychiatry, 44:*2, 92-106.

Angermeyer, M., Holzinger, A., Kilian, R., and Matschinger, H. (2001). Quality of life—as defined by schizophrenic patients and psychiatrists. *International Journal of Social Psychiatry, 47:*2, 34-42.

Bassman, R. (2001). Overcoming the impossible: My journey through schizophrenia. *Psychology Today, 34:*1, 34-40.

Bengtsson-Tops, A. and Hansson, L. (2001). Aspects of social network in schizophrenic patients living in the community. *International Journal of Social Psychiatry, 47:*3, 67-77.

Brueggemann, W. (1997). Conversation among exiles. *The Christian Century, 114,* 630-632.

Griffith, James L. and Griffith, Melissa Elliot (2002). *Encountering the Sacred in Psychotherapy.* New York: Guilford Press.

Link, B., Phelan, J., Bresnahan, M., Stueve, A., and Pescosolido, B. (1999). Public conceptions of mental illness. *American Journal of Public Health, 89:*9, 1328-1333.

Murray, J. (1998). Liberation for communion in the soteriology of Gustavo Gutierrez. *Theological Studies, 59:*1, 51-59.

Pescosolido, B., Monahan, J., Link, B., Stueve, A., and Kikuzawa, S. (1999). The public's view of competence, dangerousness and need for legal coercion of persons with mental health problems. *American Journal of Public Health, 89:*9, 1339-1345.

Soelle, D. (1985). Church: They had everything in common. *Theology Today, 42:*2, 215-219.

Tam, S., Ip, Y., Chan, C. (2000). Self-concepts of hospitalized and day-care psychiatric patients. *Journal of Social Psychology, 140:*2, 202-209.

Volf, M. (1996). *Exclusion and Embrace.* Nashville, TN: Abingdon Press.

Yamada, M., Korman, M., and Hughes, C. (2000). Predicting rehospitalization of persons with severe mental illness. *Journal of Rehabilitation, 66:*2, 32-39.

Chapter 6

McManus, K. (1999). Suffering in the theology of Edward Schillebeeckx. *Theological Studies, 60:*3, 476-491.

Teilhard de Chardin, P. (1999). Above all, trust in the slow work of God. *Pneuma, 6:*2.

Index

The Treatment of Bipolar Disorder in Pastoral Counseling

doi:10.1300/5696_10